CON[TENTS]

It's Lik[e This]

Multihulls and Multihulls, 19
*It's Hull-Shape that Counts, 20 · How Fast is Fast?, 21
· Beam instead of Ballast, 22 · Upright Comfort, 23 ·
Stability and all That, 23 · Knowing the Limits, 24
· As Safe as Can Be!, 24 · Different Boats for Different
Jobs, 25 · Loading and its Effects, 28 · Less Strain—
On Ship and Crew, 31*

2
The Advantages of Catamarans, 33
*Cruising Comfort, 33 · Upright Sailing, 34 · Time-
and-Motion Study, 34 · Unexaggerated Movements,
35 · Beam Seas and Lack of 'Pendulum' Effect, 36 ·
Comfort for all the Family, 37 · Dry Sailing and a
Sane Saloon, 38 · Kids on the Same Level, 38 · Safe
Family Sailing, 40 · Easier Crewing, 40 · Simpler Sail
Handling, 41 · Cats Lie Quietly Alongside, 42 ·
Steering Under Engine, 42 · Built-In Safety, 43 ·
Built-In Buoyancy, 43 · Shoal-Draft Advantages—In
Pilotage, 44 · Shoal-Draft Sailing and Anchoring, 45 ·
Shallow Draft at Sea, 46*

3
The Disadvantages of Catamarans, 49
*Lightness, 49 · Jerky Motion, 51 · Excess Speed
Dangers, 52 · Critical Sail Areas, 53 · The Business of
Capsizing, 54 · Golden Rule, 55 · Handling Require-
ments in Bad Weather, 55 · Space on Deck, 56 ·
Disadvantages Below Decks, 56 · Headroom on the
Bridgedeck, 57 · Visibility from Without, 57 · Berth-
ing Dues, 57 · Manoeuvring Problems Under Power,
58 · Fore and Aft Motion—and the 'Side Wallop' 59*

CONTENTS

ILLUSTRATIONS

It's Like This . . .

For two slim hulls, and the five members of the Andrews
family, another happy cruise in Scottish waters was drawing to a close. Five hundred-odd miles had slipped effort-
lessly under the bridgedeck, as little *Twintail* took us
smoothly from the sheltered sea-lochs and sounds, out to
the wind-swept Western Isles. Her twin wakes had sliced
across reflected mountains, soared in the ocean swells
and wriggled amongst tide-rips. Tomorrow, weather per-
mitting, she would take us sixty miles further, across the
North Channel towards the Irish Sea. Today, there was
less than half that distance to go.

'Gybe-Oh!'

Flipping her mainsail across by hand, I swung the little
catamaran round, past the ice-worn rocks of Skipness
Point. Heading down Kilbrennan Sound brought the
grey wind rushing, bracken-scented, from just abaft the
the starboard beam. At the very top of Force 4, it sent
us hurrying over dark wavelets, our finely curved bows
nodding gently as she knifed through the whitened crests.
Sliding southwards, she rode swiftly and level.

The rearing peaks of Arran Island were to port now.
They would have caused some right wicked squalls had
the wind been bent by them; but today it was the much
lower Kintyre shore to weather, and the breeze swept

heartily and more steadily over the patchily sunlit sound between the two.

'Let's boom out the jib,' I muttered to no one in particular, and locked in the self-steering vane. I got up, walked across the cockpit and up on to the side-deck. In the cabin, Judy was reading fairy-tales to our three small daughters, but on the catamaran's broad foredeck I had no need for help in rigging the whisker-pole and poking the jib out to weather. We could have carried the genoa, I supposed, but there was little point. With the children aged just two, three and four I was, as ever, wary of frightening them by having to take any sudden 'shout-making' actions.

As the sail filled and I trotted aft to trim it properly, the breeze freshened momentarily and *Twintail* raced off down a low wave-face. It was suddenly as if she was on rails – rushing forwards without any effort or stress, bolt upright and blissful. The wave she was on was left behind, and she rose, chasing the one ahead. Her speed held, the apparent wind rippling the ensign almost across her. Releasing the vane, I put the helm up a little. At once the twin wakes lengthened, to stretch further and further astern.

Judy leant towards the doorway from her seat in the saloon and grinned at me, nodding towards the girls. I looked in. Rona, the eldest, was gazing forwards through the arch in the main bulkhead. Beyond the forecabin windows the foredeck slowly dipped and rose, synchronising with the overtaken crests, and the sea glinted in the sunshine away down the sound. The younger two, Susan and Eileen, were curled sideways on the saloon cushions, their little arms resting on the seat-backs as they peered out of the side windows at the rapidly changing scenes of glen and mountain. The book lay on the table, between biscuit-crumbs and glasses of 'fizz'.

Standing up, with head and shoulders out of the hatch, Judy glanced at the sails, then at the long wake. By her elbow, the Sumlog's dial was purring busily, its needle wavering between eight and nine knots.

'Has she touched ten, yet?'

I shook my head. 'Not with the working jib. Wouldn't take much to put her there, though. Look at that, now . . . She nearly made it that time.'

'Like a cuppa?' Judy dodged below, stepping down to the galley in the starboard hull. *Definitely* the most understanding shipmate in the world. As she put the kettle on, *Twintail* shot off on another surging swoop, and the log needle climbed.

'There you are!' I called. 'There's your ten. Pity you didn't see it!'

'I'll see it again,' she replied.

I knew she would, even though we never drove our 'Holiday flat afloat' (as someone had rudely called her) very hard when the kids were on board. This, however, was the sort of wind which seemed set to give the 27-foot Prout Ranger a fast, easy and completely comfortable reach for all of the remaining twenty miles down to Campbeltown Loch. And at this rate, we would be there by lunch-time. We'd berth as usual in the least crowded spot, up at the shallow inner end of the harbour, where deeper craft could not lie afloat.

Sitting at ease, the helm light in my hand and the ship flying straight and true, I thought of the number of times I had made this passage from up in Loch Fyne, in similar-sized *single*-hulled yachts; and of how often it was supper-time or long past it, before we made port. Why, even if this good wind were to drop, well, at least most of us could sit in sheltered comfort round the cabin table for lunch, as we normally did at sea in *Twintail*. It had to be very rough indeed before things began to slide around at all. Not that there was any shortage of room out in her big cockpit—but today the wind was cold.

She accelerated suddenly in an even harder puff ... It was for all the world like sledging down a long, undulating hill on good crisp snow. Thrilling, unending, and delightful.

Sunshine. Land's End and the Longships, sleepily brown in the haze ahead. A flat, pale blue sea, disturbed by only a few tidal swirls.

Aku-Aku had never seen anything like it. I was delivering her, all new and sparkling, from Christchurch in Hampshire up to our home port on Loch Fyne. So far, we had had fog and calm; darkness and wind (with rain); strong headwinds and viciously steep English Channel seas over which she had shouldered her way, bucking and bouncing, with the rigging howling and the spray-hood shuddering above the recessed steering position at the fore end of the cockpit. Under its snug protection the helmsman had sat turning the wheel a little this way and that while he learnt how she liked you to bear away as she topped the crests of a big one, take it sideways, then luff her smartly as she whizzed down the back of it.

We'd had days in harbour with gales whipping coal-dust into everything, and oil smearing our snowy topsides. We had charged into Falmouth at eleven knots before a rising gale; burst a batten pocket when reefing off the Lizard, and continued to Penzance close-hauled under working jib.

But now it was all different. Catalac No. 7 was having

her nine-metre length shown just what cruising really can be. Up ahead of her blue mainsail for the very first time curved a vast yellow ghosting sail, full of an air we could barely feel. Four knots on the Sumlog lifted to $4\frac{1}{2}$ as Mike eased the wheel a little. We came about south of the Longships Light, and settled her close-hauled on port tack, her high bows searching for the Irish Sea. Mike shook his head, and grinned over his shoulder to where I sat, leaning back against the teak taffrail in a corner of the enormous cockpit.

'Don't ever tell me again,' he said, 'that catamarans won't go to windward!'

'I never did tell you that,' I replied. (Far be it from me, of all people...)

'Well, someone did. Look at that, now; hardly a ripple, and she's doing five at times. You are converting me, after all! I'll be a cat-man yet!'

'Catamariner.'

'That too.'

We changed the big sail for the genoa before dusk, but during that cold, starlit night the wind remained light, backing a little as we crossed the Bristol Channel, and *Aku-Aku* reeled off five and six knots all the way. Late next morning we sighted our only bit of Wales (the top of the Smalls Lighthouse) and altered course for the Tusker Rock, off Ireland's SE corner. Force 2 WSW, sometimes 3; never more. In the first full twenty-four hours we had averaged 5.3 knots.

The Tusker came abeam at 16.40 and, with the wind now free, we were fairly surging along, though it wasn't any stronger. Night came, and total blackness was intensified by heavy drizzle as we swept past the Codling L.V. at 03.00. She winked her decklights at us; a friendly greeting out of the dark nowhere.

My crew were asleep below—one in the quarter cabin, and one in the saloon, a comfortable shape with nodding head, hunched in a rounded corner of the big settee. As I glanced through the doorway, the lightship's receding beam showed me an unstarted mug of cocoa standing unattended on the Formica-topped cabin table near his elbow. I slipped off the helmsman's chair, ducked in quietly, and jotted a brief entry in the log-book, noting the change of course. The mug felt warm still—shame to let it go cold undrunk . . .

The dawn brought improved wind-strength, Force 4, just, but poor vis.; not that that mattered much, with over a hundred miles to go. The twenty-four hour run this time was 5.99 knots, but that didn't last. By the following midnight we were utterly becalmed in the entrance to the Firth of Clyde! The new morning sun, however, found the ghoster at work again as the familiar Kintyre coastline formed itself out of the haze, and we were soon heading up-loch among the green, Highland hills. All but four hundred miles in a mite under three days . . . Clearly my crew were enthralled.

In such very gentle conditions, with a waterline length of under twenty-five feet, our over-all average of 5.4 knots was astonishing, even to me.

As we stowed sails and started the engine for the last few yards to our berth, someone said, 'It'll take a motor-yacht to better that average in the same light winds —and they *roll*!'

I

Multihulls and Multihulls

Somebody once wrote (in a journal called *The Sailorman*) that there were really only three types of boat:

> Half a Catamaran (1 hull),
> A Catamaran (2 hulls), and
> A Catamaran And A Half (3 hulls).

Maybe thoroughly flippant, but not without some sense, when you think about it.

The choice of any boat depends naturally on many things; what accommodation is required, what sort of sailing (cruising or racing) you like to do, and what amount of money you are prepared to spend in order to get it. These are only a few of them. On average, however, it does appear that for a given sum, a catamaran may provide more accommodation, and almost certainly more 'boat' than any other type. The reason for this is that their construction can be kept remarkably uncomplicated, and there is usually no costly ballast keel to bump up the price.

Everyone is used to the idea of single-hulled boats having evolved into many distinct forms, some being ideal mainly for cruiser-racing, others for creek crawling, some for slow sturdiness at sea, for trailing behind the family car to new cruising grounds, and so on. (This book is not concerned with dinghy types.) But curiously, many people tend to think of 'multihulls' as being all one kind of thing. *This is definitely not the case.* There is every bit as much difference between the 'double-canoe' (catamaran) and the single-canoe with twin outriggers (trimaran), as there is between either of them and a monohull or even the very rare single-outrigger canoe (proa) type, such as the famous Transatlantic racer *Cheers*.

Although the modern form of the general multihull idea is quite a recent development, the cruising versions of each kind have evolved separately into distinctly 'classifiable' shapes; and since this book is about catamarans, it is the several and various forms of catamaran which I want to discuss.

IT'S HULL-SHAPE THAT COUNTS

In these days of mass-production, the development of multihulled craft is to some extent retarded, because relatively few people can afford to have their 'cat' or 'tri' designed and built as a 'one off' job, simply to suit their own personal ideas and preferences. Most of us are forced by our finances to buy what is readily available.

But far worse is the fact that many a multihull has been bought solely because the advertising said she was 'fast', or simply because she had the sort of living accommodation that the buyer required, or was particularly cheap to build. And yet, although such boats are for the most part unballasted, and therefore rely very largely indeed on rig and hull-shape to behave safely in adverse conditions, or even to perform well in light winds, people only rarely seem to give the *type of hull* they are buying any great consideration. Yet that hull-shape, as I will try to show in some detail, is what will really decide whether the boat one chooses is likely to suit family pottering, off-shore racing, ocean cruising, or whatever is most intended by her owner.

HOW FAST IS FAST?

As a quick example, let us glance at the business of speed. Not all catamarans are fast, just as not all monohulls are fast. Speed depends on many aspects of design, and on how owners are going to load the different kinds of hull. Some owners want speed in light conditions; others prefer their craft to be at their best in a stiff breeze.

Quite apart from shape, in order to achieve speed through the water, a sailing boat must either carry a great press of sail, or be kept very light. If she is to carry a lot of sail, something obviously has to be provided to counteract the wind's efforts to blow her over sideways and capsize her. Most single-hulled boats manage this by the addition of heavy ballast carried low down, either in the bottom of the hull or, as is the modern practice, at the bottom of a deep fin keel, in which case the weight needed is less, because of the better leverage involved. But either way, you end up with a boat which has little *initial* stability, but which becomes stiffer and stiffer as she is forced over, so that she will right herself at once should she ever be knocked flat by wind or wave.

The snag is that these boats will normally sail at an angle of heel proportional to the wind-strength, and the amount of sail carried. Unfortunately, the more sail carried, the more the need for more ballast, and the more ballast, the greater the underwater drag, so the more the need for even more sail to drive it. Most monohulls also tend to roll badly when the wind is on or abaft the beam, due to wind and wave action having a 'pendulum' effect on their ballast keels and easily heeled hulls. And lastly, if ever seriously holed by sudden contact with something big and solid, a ballasted boat is more than likely to sink rapidly.

A multihulled boat, on the other hand, can achieve the counterbalancing of the wind's heeling effects, up to a very great extent, without any ballast at all, and it is largely this factor which enables her, *in the right conditions,* to sail a lot faster than a monohull of the same length. In other words, her 'power/weight ratio' is infinitely better than that of a ballasted boat. The idea is quite simply to provide a wide base (like the wheelbase of a car, as compared to that of a motor-cycle) so that the wind cannot easily blow her over sideways, nor yet even heel her to any marked degree. The sails are thus forced to convert practically all their effort *instantly* into moving her forwards.

So why not just have a very beamy monohull—like a big dinghy? Because it has long been known that speed through water is diminished by the width of the vessel in relation to her length. In other words, a very narrow canoe-like boat, say ten metres (33 feet) long, is going to have a much higher speed potential than a beamier version the same length. The amount of sail that can be carried has really not much to do with it, because in the long run it is the wave-making which puts the brakes on—and your long slim hull makes hardly any waves in comparison to her big fat sister. So whereas if you gave a ten-metre monohull a beam of maybe 4½ metres (say, fifteen or sixteen feet) she would sail like a cow and get nowhere slowly, the catamaran with those overall dimensions streaks away at speed, simply because although she has *two* hulls to push through the water, they can both be of a very slim, low-drag (low wave-making) shape.

UPRIGHT COMFORT

The advantages are obvious. A catamaran, for instance, apart from often being able to make faster, easier passages than similar-sized monohulled craft, provides a platform which remains relatively level in all but the most dire conditions, and is therefore more comfortable and less tiring to live in at sea. She will not heel (nor roll) much over eight or ten degrees beyond the angle of the water surface, and her initial stability is immense. (Trimarans heel considerably further than catamarans.)

It has become quite clear that catamarans have no need of deep fixed keels, and can therefore be beached in shallow water on their own bottoms without the need for fancy cradles, posts or 'legs' to hold them upright— a most useful attribute in today's crowded anchorages. The ability of many catamarans to sail to windward in extremely shoal water without loss of performance is another happy advantage.

STABILITY AND ALL THAT...

The snags of such a boat may be pretty obvious too, some of them, but the one which immediately springs to the minds of most people is that of what is termed 'ultimate stability'. Being lightly built and unballasted, most multihulls can theoretically be capsized, in certain circumstances. Therefore, the thing one has to decide when considering buying a multihull, is just what importance to place on that fact. And naturally, a lot is going to depend on the particular design of the boat you have in mind.

It is, I think, worth remembering that people have been sailing large and small unballasted *mono*hulls for centuries, without frequent disasters. One has only to think of the ocean-going Viking longships, quite apart from the more recent sailing-barge type of craft. The stately Thames Spritsail Barges often made coastal passages without any cargo or ballast on board, and I have no doubt could then be capsized, just as could many Dutch Barges or the English Barge-Yacht variation *and a good deal more easily than many similar-sized multihulled yachts of today.*

KNOWING THE LIMITS

The reason that such sailing barges hardly *ever* went over is simply because those who sailed them *knew and respected their limits.* Any fool could have a Thames Barge over in a strong breeze provided the gear held together and he held on to full sail. But bargemen know very well not to do that, and don't.

So it is—or should be—with multihulled yachts.

AS SAFE AS CAN BE!

It is my firm belief that once you understand and respect the stability margins and the forces involved in a well designed and properly constructed catamaran, as opposed to other types of mono- or multihull yacht, she becomes one of the safest small boats man has ever devised, especially when fitted with adequate built-in buoyancy to render her unsinkable even if totally flooded.

Why, you may well ask, should I apply this statement to *twin*-hulled craft in particular?

Well, in my own experience so far (having cruised several thousands of sea miles in widely assorted craft both with and without my young family, and having 'sail-tested' many new multihull designs in the course of my work as a sailing journalist), and also in the wider experience of others who have crossed the great oceans, the catamaran appears to be less wearing on her crew, less sick-making, less given to violent motion (in short, less difficult to exist in), than the vast majority of single-hulled yachts or trimarans.

If that is so, why then do so many people persist in sailing monohulls and trimarans? Why, even I myself have been known to state that there are few things more delightful to steer to windward than a well-balanced, well-tuned sailing monohull. Usually in the same breath I then add that most multihulls are far more pleasant to steer downwind, partly because the risk of gybing is minimised by the complete absence of rolling. But the point is of course that fortunately everyone has his or her own personal likes and dislikes. It is all a matter of what each individual requires and expects of a boat—a matter of the kind of sailing he or she most wishes to do.

DIFFERENT BOATS FOR DIFFERENT JOBS

If one simply wants a boat which will look after her crew when they have become exhausted by severe conditions, a monohull is likely to be a better choice than most multihulls. One *can* get away with carrying too much sail in a monohull, in that most of them are self-righting. But there is no doubt that although safer from that point of view, in virtually all weather conditions they are much less comfortable, and far more tiring to crew than are multihulls.

If one is looking for sheer speed and has no need for lots of accommodation or weight-carrying ability, a properly designed and built trimaran might well be the thing for you. The gigantic French trimaran *Pen Duick IV* has proved just what her type is capable of, *if* constructed correctly to meet the stresses and strains involved in dashing across the oceans at high speed under all conditions—but surely in her case at any rate no one could say she is pretty or anything less than extremely cumbersome in port.

From the true cruising point of view, the loading of gear, food and water etc. into a trimaran whose wing floats are buoyant enough not to be easily depressed, must be done with infinite care and caution. The Piver designed 40-foot Victress trimaran so expertly sailed solo around the world by Nigel Tetley eventually destroyed herself completely while still at sea, and she is alas only one of many trimarans broken up by the continual wracking, twisting and fluctuating strains occasioned by being heavily laden in big seas. The fact that *Victress*'s troubles began when relatively few days out at the beginning of her voyage emphasises the root cause. (Admittedly she was not a new ship, but that should not have made much difference. Plenty of extremely elderly boats have safely sailed the oceans.)

It would seem, from this and other recorded incidents, that both from the apparently unpredictable danger of tripping over the lee float's bow and so capsizing, and from the difficulties associated with loading, the trimaran concept often has disadvantages when used for long-distance cruising. Naturally, if one keeps them light there is no problem—but how do you keep an ocean cruiser light? Anyway, I am talking in a very general sense, and the above sweeping statements should not be taken as applying to all, or anything like all, makes of trimaran. *Of course* safely designed trimarans have and are being built. A favourite of mine is Honnor Marine's John Westell designed Ocean Bird 'swing-wing' version, for I have seen none that I consider more seaworthy or better thought-out from a cruising point of view. Another, smaller trimaran I also like a lot is A.J.S Sandwich Yacht Construction Ltd.'s Telstar eight-metre folding-wing trailable cruiser, which combines the ability to cruise with a phenomenal racing performance. But she is hardly an 'ocean cruiser', nor intended as such.

Correctly speaking, a trimaran is a 'double-outrigger canoe', and the aim of its wing floats is therefore only to provide lateral or 'straddle' stability for its main and central hull, thus taking the place of ballast. The floats are nowadays not normally designed to be truly load-bearing, and so usually can be totally immersed if the craft is overpressed. In normal, fresh conditions, when beating, most trimarans are likely to heel to as much as fifteen degrees or so—roughly fifty per cent more than will the average catamaran in the same breeze. If the tri's wing floats *can't* be immersed because they are big enough and buoyant enough to be able individually to support almost the entire weight of the boat, then it seems to me that you might just as well have a catamaran in the first place, and save the expense of one hull, *and* the embarrassment of such vast overall width when in harbour, and wind up with better accommodation into the bargain.

Suppose we look at it this way: A catamaran of just under thirty feet overall length (nine metres) offers the amount of accommodation which, for example, my own family (five of us) requires, within a reasonably compact beam of fourteen feet (4.27 metres). She also provides a layout giving greater general space and privacy than is possible in any trimaran of the same overall length and price, which would in any event have a beam of something like eighteen feet or even more.

I confess there are some trimarans I have greatly enjoyed sailing. Moreover, at one time I believed that the trimaran configuration might possibly constitute a safer seaboat than the catamaran in really extreme conditions. For that reason, I have delved into the matter of safety at sea very carefully indeed, but am now confident that the reverse is more likely to be true, and for some extremely good reasons, which were not all apparent to begin with.

LOADING AND ITS EFFECTS

With a catamaran, the problems of loading and consequent effects on her structure at sea, are not the same nor as difficult to overcome as in a trimaran, for the simple reason that she has only two hulls, and these can act together on the wave-surface much more easily than can three hulls.

Three hulls in a short beam sea, for example, produce a repeating situation where two of them are being irregularly and rapidly lifted by crests whilst the central hull (or one of the wings) is left to some extent 'hanging' in or over the trough. Then within seconds, the wave has moved on by one hull, as it were, and the central float is suddenly lifted while the first float is deprived of supporting water.

When going hard to windward, even in a long ocean

type of sea (never mind the often much more vicious coastal seas) this changing, one-up, two-down, two-up, one-down effect is sorely aggravated. A fierce diagonal twisting also may simultaneously occur, where the bow of, say, the lee float is being strongly lifted at the same moment as its own stern may be relatively unsupported over a trough, and the stern of the opposite wing float is perhaps being lifted. The buffetting effect when sailing at speed can be truly terrible, and this diagonal straining is carried at least over into the main hull by the connecting structure, if not indeed over the entire craft.

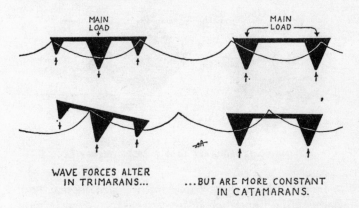

WAVE FORCES ALTER
IN TRIMARANS...   ...BUT ARE MORE CONSTANT
                             IN CATAMARANS.

I am often asked how I feel about the 'terrible toll which the 1968 Observer Single-Handed Transatlantic Race took on multihulls'. Certainly, several ill-conceived multihulls broke up, but there are two points which must be remembered. Firstly, multihulls in general were at a noticeably less advanced stage of development then than now, and the craft which were crippled were largely experimental. In those days, the boats taking part did not have to do a qualifying course first. Secondly, the vast

majority of those in trouble were trimarans, not catamarans. Of the cats which gave up, one was an uncom-
pleted, untried, one-off design which had a rudder
failure; and the other, a production boat, lost her mast
simply because a rigger had fitted the wrong size of in-
sulators in her backstays, which doubled as transmitting
aerials. She made her way home, jury rigged, without
assistance. Neither craft suffered hull or bridgedeck
damage, which alas cannot be said of the several trimarans in the race, some of which disintegrated altogether.

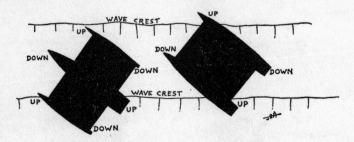

TWISTING STRAINS ARE LESS COMPLICATED IN A CAT.

In the case of those trimarans designed so that both
floats act buoyantly when the vessel is at rest (as in most
Piver designs, for instance) the twisting at sea may at most
be imposed over the entire yacht from side to side, especially when deeply laden. However, trimarans designed
to float, even when at rest, with one wing float clear of
or barely touching the water (and therefore which sail
with one leg almost perpetually waving in the air), are
to some extent less troubled by diagonal twisting of
this kind. They become indeed 'a catamaran and a half'.
Two floats bear the weight, and one just hangs around,

being useful solely as ballast. The drawbacks of hanging ballast out to windward at the end of an outrigger are that it is still subjected to jerking strains due to the movements of the rest of the craft, and, when one remembers this is 'ballast' of the kind strong enough and bulky enough to support the boat when it reverts to being a mere float, there is also the impressive windage (air-drag) created by its necessary size and connecting structure. And as unfortunately proved in some number of cases where the windage was considerable, due to wing decks, this factor has actively assisted trimarans to capsize both at sea and at moorings.

WINDAGE

I have no wish at all to decry trimarans—nor indeed monohulls; I merely want to compare the *differences* between those types of boat and catamarans.

LESS STRAIN—ON SHIP AND CREW

In a catamaran, the strains on the structure are less complicated, and will be discussed at length in the chapter on hull-shapes and construction. Obviously cats have their drawbacks too, and I will also try to make these especially clear. I have no axe to grind, by the way; I have no connection of any kind, nor have ever had, with any catamaran marketing organisation, builder, or designer. However, having had my share of sailing in a wide variety of craft, I have become far more intrigued by multihulls than by 'conventional' yachts, for certain purposes, and by catamarans in particular, since to me they seem more practical than anything else for cruising in comfort.

As a family, we have turned from monohulls to catamarans for cruising, simply because we think them safe, more comfortable at sea, a little faster, and ideal for exploring shallow waters and drying out on beaches and creek-beds. In the following chapters I will try to reason out objectively just why we believe these claims to be true.

2

The Advantages of
Catamarans

The two main advantages of the double-canoe type of craft are generally reckoned as Comfort and Speed, in that order. Much past advertising has claimed speed as the major factor, and it has been well and truly proved that some catamarans at least are indeed very much faster round a given course than monohulls of the same waterline length. Fair enough. But from the cruising man's point of view, with maybe just his wife (and the young family she may have constantly to attend to) on board, comfort is the prime factor, and speeds beyond those of a good fast monohull of the same length are seldom going to be reached—if the boat is sailed really wisely. Even so, one will find that catamarans tend to be a lot faster at cruising than they are at racing—a curious fact which I will explain in a moment. But, for sheer *comfort* at sea there is nothing so suitable for cruising in as the well designed catamaran.

CRUISING COMFORT

Comfort in a small boat is relative anyway, but it is nevertheless made up of many things. It is more than just comfortable bunks and an uncramped cabin. It is more than an easy motion in a seaway, too. But it *is* something which catamarans have to offer in a degree which no other type of sailing boat can match. Why? Well, let's look at what might be called the Components of Catamaran Comfort.

UPRIGHT SAILING

The most obvious point is that most catamarans will heel no more than a normal maximum of eight or ten degrees to the water surface. The sloping face of a wave must of course be added to that if the length of the wave-face is as great or greater than the overall beam of the catamaran, assuming she is sailing roughly at right-angles to the true wind. This means that in conditions up to around Force 6 it is possible to put, for instance, a mug of coffee down on the cabin table without the need for fiddle-rails to keep it there, and without it spilling.

TIME-AND-MOTION STUDY

When Judy and I bought our first cruising catamaran, she discovered that galley jobs which would have taken maybe twenty minutes to prepare because of the motion and angle of heel of the sturdy, conventional eight-ton ketch we had been used to, now took less than half the time in the same wind and sea conditions. This was simply because everything she put down did *not* have to be wedged carefully in place before she let go of it. Even on a Formica surface in the catamaran, things tended to stay where she put them, more or less, despite whatever sea was running, or the press of wind in the sails. That particular catamaran, a 27-foot Prout Ranger called *Twintail,* hardly ever heeled much beyond eight degrees except with the help of steep, beam seas—and yet by modern cat standards she was exceptionally narrow.

UNEXAGGERATED MOVEMENTS

Admittedly the motion of most catamarans is very rapid, partly because they are so light and buoyant, and partly because of the way, even in beam-on conditions, they are affected by the oncoming seas; but I shall go into this in detail in the chapters on Sea-keeping and on Safety.

The fact remains, though, that this quick but unexaggerated type of motion inherent in the double-canoe configuration is noticeably far less tiring than the varying, sometimes considerable angles of heel and roll of a monohull in the same conditions. I have always put this down to the fact that since the actual movements of a catamaran are so much *smaller* than those of a conventional yacht, one's body does not have to struggle for so long with each separate movement, before a counteracting movement comes to relieve its muscles.

In the days when I sailed in a surprisingly varied succession of monohulled vessels, it was always necessary, before getting under way, to 'stow for sea'. Anything movable, from bedding-rolls to books, crockery to cameras, or pans to parallel rulers, had to be secured in place to allow for the rolling or heeling which was almost sure to come in anything of a breeze. Overall, I must have spent many hours of otherwise good sailing time chocking items away so that they wouldn't come crashing out when someone opened, say, the jam locker on the windward side. Even then, on our very first cruise together, in a pretty staid Maurice Griffiths heavy-displacement monohull, my wife sustained severe bruising (and was lucky at that) when a pile of biscuit tins cascaded out of a locker which we all thought had been properly stowed.

I wonder how many catamaran owners start their preparations to get under way by 'stowing for sea'. Most of us, I would think, simply cast off the sail-tyers and get going. It will have to be very rough indeed before things start sliding off tables and shelves, and something really awful will have happened if anything jumps out of a locker!

I have photographic evidence of a 'house' of playing-cards built by one of my daughters on the cabin table of our nine metre Catalac, which stood without falling during a $3\frac{1}{2}$-mile beat across Loch Fyne while the ship was travelling at six knots in a Force 3 wind. This rather knocks the well-known 'milk bottle' story into a cocked hat!

But to the point: Around coastal waters, the angle of the face of seas is not normally very great, even in bad conditions. It is usually even less off-shore. For that reason, I have never seen the inclinometer of any catamaran being sailed with both hulls in the water exceed twenty-eight degrees. In relation to the wave surface, most trimarans will nearly double the heel angle of most catamarans, while the average monohull may frequently be heeled to angles beyond fifty degrees off the vertical. It does not take much imagination, quite apart from actual experience, to envisage what it can be like trying to cook, sit, or even lie down in a boat which is not only repeatedly going over to that sort of angle, but leaping up and down as well.

BEAM SEAS AND LACK OF 'PENDULUM' EFFECT

People often wonder what will happen when you take a catamaran out into a really big, steep, beam-on sea. Well, don't let anyone tell you that catamarans never roll, if 'roll' is the nautical term used to describe a repeated heeling from one side to the other. Indeed they will 'roll', provided the sea is steep enough and large enough to lift first one hull, and while dropping it, pass below the boat and lift the opposite hull. Naturally in those conditions, the masthead of even a catamaran will swing rapidly from side to side, but *she will never swing much beyond the angle of the wave-face* (plus her own sailing angle), as will a monohull with her heavy pendulum of a ballast keel.

So not only is the motion itself less tiring, since the boat continues to sail pretty well upright all the time regardless of wind strength or direction, but what motion there is, being quick rather than like the slow, hesitant roll of a monohull, is very noticeably less nauseating. I know quite a number of folk who were frequently ill at sea in monohulls and who find themselves only extremely rarely so affected in catamarans. To me, that is a very *definite* advantage!

COMFORT FOR ALL THE FAMILY

All this means that those not only on watch, but those off watch as well, are liable to remain much more relaxed than in other kinds of boat. By a stroke of extraordinary good fortune, my study window happens to look out on an area just outside the entrance to one of the most popular harbours in the West of Scotland. While 'thinking' during the course of my work, my eye is often distracted (most pleasantly) by yachts on passage up or down the big sea loch, and I cannot help noticing how, on cold, blustery or wet days, the entire crews of monohulls tend to be huddled together out in the cramped, spray-lashed confines of their small and often badly exposed cockpits, cocooned in oilskins and hanging grimly to the weather (or lee) coamings in chilled and dampened apparent misery. (I recall doing the same sort of thing myself.) The 'joys of yachting', it is called, and is done in preference to being cooped up in a long cabin lying over on its side, whose small windows would show on the one hand only the racing water, and on the other how grey and lowering the sky was. Down there, one could only attempt to take one's ease on a seat or bunk placed at an ever altering and seldom anything but comfortable angle of heel.

DRY SAILING AND A SANE SALOON

The contrast is all too clear when a catamaran slides into sight, barely heeling, and throwing next to no spray on deck. When it is raining or too cold for her crew to be disporting themselves in her wide and roomy cockpit, the catamaran's helmsman at least can sit there in relative comfort on an upright seat, with no one jogging his elbow or tripping over his feet. Just inside the cabin door, his family or friends can meantime sit cosily dry and out of the wind, round the cabin table. From there they can watch through the windows other craft and such passing scenery as is visible through the rain, and yet can remain completely in touch with what is going on, ready (one hopes) to lend a hand instantly if needed. (No companion ladders to bark their shins on in a quick exit.)

KIDS ON THE SAME LEVEL

No longer is the accommodation necessarily described as 'down below', for much of it will be on the same bridge-deck level as the cockpit itself, and this has very special advantages indeed, where young children are concerned. In constant communication with Mum and Dad in the cockpit (unless the door is shut on them in desperation), yet with a virtually horizontal table to play at, and probably an all-round view through the big windows, kids do not have that 'shut away' feeling imposed by being bundled down into a deep single hull. From the majority of monohulls' cabins there is often little to see but the moving, swinging clouds, and occasional glimpses of Mum's head and shoulders in the companionway, as she changes sides and hauls on ropes (with ensuing metallic ringing or grating of the sheet-winch mechanisms), when Dad puts the helm over and their whole world suddenly pitches over from one side, away round and down, on to the other.

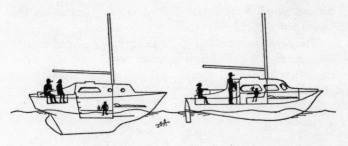

CHILD'S EYE-LEVEL IN MONOHULLS & CATAMARANS.

In a catamaran there is still the scream or clatter of the winches, of course, but people 'below' decks can *see* that the boat is turning, and that Dad and Mum are doing things with the sails. They can *see* where the craft is now heading, and how she rises to the oncoming seas and soars lightly over them. Or the kids can go down into one of the hulls if they want, to play in a secure bunk which is extremely unlikely even in severe conditions to cant over suddenly and tip them out.

SAFE FAMILY SAILING

Furthermore, from their control positions in the cockpit, parents can usually see that their offspring are happily playing (or squabbling about the crayons or whatever), and can, without more than the usual difficulty, call their attention to some passing scene. And the children can then pause, glance up at whatever it is, and get on with what *really* interests them at that moment, without having to leave their seat at the table unless they want to. Or, in a catamaran, they can go out and play with complete safety within the spacious confines of a broad cockpit floor or deck, without necessarily getting tangled up in and inadvertently releasing the sheets from their jam-cleats.

Either way, there can be little genuine arguing with the fact that a catamaran is a far better and safer craft for folk with really young families than any other kinds of sailing boat.

EASIER CREWING

As far as an adult crew are concerned, steering a catamaran is for some reason a lot less tiring than steering a comparable monohull. (It can, in some designs, be rather less interesting, too.) Crewing in general is very much easier—and safer. The usually large cockpit makes for easy work at the sheets, helps to keep uncoiled ends from tangling between tacks, leaves plenty of elbow-room for the helmsman, and allows everyone to stretch out in a fair state of relaxation between bursts of activity.

Deck work in a catamaran is where one reaps the real advantages over those on the heeling, narrow and often cluttered decks of a monohull; particularly up forward. Where even trimarans come to a point by the forestay, most catamarans have a wide, open space almost as broad as the full beam of the boat, from which to hoist and lower the headsails. Spinnakers, when they are carried, loose much of their horrors with a broad working surface below them on which the crew can dance the Battle of the Boom.

Admittedly in some catamarans this space between the bows is 'decked over', not with solid planking or GRP, but with a big net of webbing or light line appropriately known as a 'trampoline', and on which toes have to be operated with care; but they do mean that even then one can move around safely, and lowered sails will mostly end up there, rather than overside.

SIMPLER SAIL HANDLING

In my own catamarans I have rarely found it necessary to 'gather' a headsail while lowering it, because even when the wind is abaft the beam, the sheet will usually retain the sail inside the width of the boat, so not even the biggest headsail tends to land outside the rail as it comes down.

Foredeck work in a monohull or a narrow foredecked trimaran is neither easy nor safe—in a catamaran the problems are very minor, so her needs can readily be attended to, even in rough water. The business of actually *going* forward (or returning aft to the cockpit) is much easier on an upright deck—almost as easy at sea as in port. This is hardly the case in a boat which heels, where the cabintop handrail on the weather side may suddenly be lower than your feet, or so that on the lee side, your feet may be immersed in inches of icy, fast-flowing water while you fight your way past the rigging.

The process of reefing is also greatly eased in an up-right-sailing catamaran. The cabintop is not (one sin-cerely hopes) going to suddenly heel away over so that you have to stop and hold on. Certainly its vertical move-ment may be enough to make the wearing of safety har-ness an extremely good idea in bad weather, but generally speaking, reefing is not half the battle I have known it be in a boat which heels.

CATS LIE QUIETLY ALONGSIDE

And when the harbour has been gained, a further advan-tage becomes noticeable (particularly in canal locks). As opposed to the rounded curve of topsides and rail occa-sioned by the beam of a monohull which reduces naturally to a point at the bow and a narrowing at her stern, most catamarans are relatively straight-sided, and so lie alongside a dock wall or pontoon quietly and steadily, with no tendency to swing about. Usually only three fenders will be required to protect the topside.

STEERING UNDER ENGINE

Manoeuvrability under power in a catamaran fitted either with an outboard motor which can be turned even a little to either side, or in one fitted with twin inboard engines or twin propellers, is excellent. And whereas a ballasted monohull will 'carry her way' in neutral (and consequently may be hard to stop, because of her considerable momentum) a cat can usually be pulled up or accelerated forwards with fair ease. Furthermore, the lack of momentum of such light-weight craft also means that should some awful error occur (it happens to most of us—the engine fails, or the helmsman misjudges or mistimes), the resulting bump, if alas there is one, will be nothing like so hard or damaging as would have been the case in a heavy, ballasted boat.

BUILT-IN SAFETY

Although catamarans can, as I have said, be made to capsize, (and this aspect will be fully dealt with later in the book) people with considerable multihull experience (including one or two who *have* actually inverted their their boats) are of the convinced opinion that taken all in all, a good catamaran is likely to be *far safer* than other forms of yacht. To quote Dr David Lewis, who sailed the forty-foot Mudie-designed, Prout built, *Rehu Moana* round the world with his family:

'I can only conclude from our experiences that a well designed catamaran is faster, roomier, much more convenient and spacious and probably safer than a conventional yacht.'

I have not his knowledge of ocean sailing, and therefore can add nothing to that, but I have some thousands of miles of coastal and what might reasonably be termed 'off-shore' sailing astern of me, and know how on many, many occasions, I have been very glad indeed of the advantages offered by catamarans.

BUILT-IN BUOYANCY

Not every cat is fitted with full buoyancy, though this can fairly easily be done by their owners, if not by their builders. And then, with the lack of dead-weight ballast, even if she were to fill due to collision with some floating object on a dark night or by some other means, your catamaran will not sink. Even if one was silly enough to make her capsize, she would still be there, however uncomfortable, on the surface. How many keel-boat crews can say the same of their craft?

And suppose one found it absolutely imperative to run her ashore? Since even a large catamaran will sail in two or three feet (less than a metre) of water, any suitable beach could be reached safely, and, with luck, very little damage done, even in surf. Not the sort of action I'd recommend, except in extremely dire emergencies, of course!

SHOAL-DRAFT ADVANTAGES—IN PILOTAGE

There is considerable safety from the pilotage angle too. I remember my first catamaran trip along the South Coast of England (in thick haze with an inaccurate distance recorder). We had made an overnight passage down Channel from Folkestone, rounding Beachy Head in the early hours, and had dodged inshore to be out of the main shipping lane. In those days there was no 'traffic routing' for the big boys, and one simply took one's chance.

With our lack of local knowledge, we failed to appreciate that a tidal set had during the misty morning taken us even further in-shore, and by lunch-time were not a little intrigued when we found ourselves amidst a rash of lobster-pot floats where none should be. No land was in sight, but rapid consultation with the echo-sounder showed a lot less than four feet under our hulls. (It was LW Springs, with a high barometer just to make things worse.)

With drop-keels raised to avoid contact with the lobsters themselves, we slid on and over the Owers Banks without mishap, and I have often thought since how hard we might have struck had we been navigating a deep-keeled, conventional yacht. Granted, we had no business to be there, and I am not proud of the incident, but these things *do* happen now and then, to at least some of us. Because we were sailing a cat, we got away with it, though we certainly did not deserve to.

I recall a similar incident among the 'pladdies' (boulder shoals) of multi-islanded Strangford Lough in Northern Ireland, some years back. Fine day, with a brisk breeze and strong sun. Water all rippling and glittering, so you couldn't see the floating weed-heads ... Guests on board, and the skipper pointing out the seals and seal-cubs instead of attending to the chart. *Twintail* was making well over six knots, with the wind abeam, roaring up the sunpath.

And suddenly we were over it, with brown bladder-wrack all round us and our hearts up and choking us. Again, and *only* because our cat was so light-drafted and shallow, we got out and over and away without a single bump—and what a bump it *might* have been, for we clearly saw some of those boulders!

SHOAL-DRAFT SAILING AND ANCHORING

This same facility of being able to sail, even to windward, in very shallow water, also means that when a deeper boat might be forced on entering a crowded anchorage to come to her hook in a none-too-well-sheltered position, the catamaran owner can often find himself some superbly secluded spot where hardly any other boats dare go. If there is a stretch of level, clean sand

45

or mud (as, for instance, at Salcombe, Fowey, Christ-church, Chichester Harbour, and *dozens* of places in the Thames Estuary or West Country, to mention hardly any) he can bring up over that.

Most catamarans can dry out comfortably and without the slightest discomfort to her crew. This may enable one to get away from the crowd, sheltered, maybe, from some forecast gale under the nearby trees, with no one likely to drag into you or run you down in the night. Really soft mud, or mud of uneven consistency such as might well put a bilge-keel boat into trouble by letting one keel sink further than its twin, will not worry the catamaran skipper; his boat will float as well on the mud-surface as on the water which left her there.

SHALLOW DRAFT AT SEA

And at sea, in severe conditions, once more the light draft of a catamaran will come to her aid, so long as she has sea-room. Not having a deep blade hanging into the water beneath her, when a sea catches her sideways she can 'give' with it easily, riding it rather as a boxer rides a punch. Not just the shallow-draft helps her here; her lack of heavy ballast means that she can move quickly in response to the sudden thrust of the seas, where the ballasted boat firstly is slow to change direction or to accelerate or decelerate as the case may be, and then as her heavy keel is held in the denser water far below, is bowled over sideways as the crest advances.

I am not saying *all* catamarans will behave well at sea; just that from past experiences it would seem that the majority of good ones have this advantage over the majority of good monohulls. The comparison with equally light trimarans in such conditions is not so different, though it would appear that many trimarans can become bothered by their lee floats digging in.

Concisely then, the advantages of a good catamaran over other types of cruising yacht, can be listed as follows:

Space, comfort, and stability, resulting in happier, more relaxed cruising for the sea-wife, as well as for small children (or teen-age sunbathers), and for the skipper, who knows the boat is less likely to frighten or 'put off' less keen members of his crew.

Speed, (in the right conditions, great speed) shortening passage times, giving longer in port or the possibility of considerably extending one's cruising range beyond that possible in a similar-sized monohull, and the occasional advantage of being able to reach shelter in advance of a blow.

Smallest possible angle of heel, reducing crew fatigue, making the supplying of cooked meals at sea relatively easy, and making life in general easier and safer below and on deck. (Nor will a catamaran frighten those non-sailing guests by 'heeling to the breeze'.)

Reduced motion, again meaning safer working or living conditions for the crew, and at the same time reducing the risks imposed mentally and physically by sea-sickness.

Visibility from below, and easy communication with those in the cockpit, which is pleasant both for children and adults, not to mention the 'off-watch' skipper/navigator.

Easy sail changing facilitated by broad decks and little motion, combined with lack of heeling.

Good manoeuvrability under power, which needs little amplification.

Easy berthing alongside, specially useful in canals, etc.

Safety off-shore and in-shore occasioned by light draft and lack of ballast.

Shallow draft, making pilotage easier, opening out anchorages unavailable to deeper craft, and making for safety at sea in severe conditions.

Any catamaran enthusiast can, of course, at once think of many other striking advantages—but for me to elaborate any further here would only be boring. I consider the above to be the *main* advantages.

And what are the *dis*advantages? It would be criminal to ignore them, for they are, of course, equally important ... but not quite so numerous!

3

The Disadvantages of
Catamarans

Every boat is a compromise. You can't expect optimum
speed without causing inconvenience in other aspects of
the craft. You can't have weight-carrying ability without
sacrificing some speed. The most safe and stable boat
is likely to be under-canvassed in light airs. The really
shallow boat may not have the windward abilities of a
deeper one. And so on.

In comparison with single-hulled boats a catamaran
designed with cruising mainly in mind will almost certainly be faster than a true monohulled cruiser of around
the same length. And under the *right conditions* of wind
and sea, even an all-out cruising catamaran may show
a turn of speed far in excess of that possible by the best
of off-shore racing monohulls.

All this may *sound* like an advantage, which it undoubtedly is, but in order to enjoy that advantage, the
catamaran has done away with the need for ballast, and
is therefore noticeably lighter than a comparable monohull. And that very lightness produces *several* very considerable disadvantages.

LIGHTNESS

Lightness inevitably means that, for example, a catamaran will not carry her way (or 'shoot') more than a

length or two when headed into the wind. Manoeuvring and particularly tacking is thus not always just a matter of shoving the helm down, as it can be in a monohull.

In other words, in order to handle a multihull well, one has to learn a slightly different kind of sailing technique—which I shall say something about in a later chapter. It is not more difficult than monohulled keelboat sailing; just different here and there. Perhaps the best way to describe it is to say that a man who has sailed mainly in racing dinghies will find the transition to multihull skills more natural than one brought up in keel-boats. Either way, the new techniques are easily mastered. And if you *start* sailing in multihulls, there is no problem at all!

The lack of momentum in most catamarans also means that certain flukey wind conditions may be more bothersome to the cat skipper than to the keel-boat man. This may be quite a severe drawback for instance when sailing into a harbour or river-mouth, where buildings or trees may create 'dead' patches or unexpectedly directioned squalls. A catamaran stops when the wind stops, and may try to accelerate violently forwards (or even backwards) when her skipper least wants or expects her to do so. The 'catamariner', as he has been termed, has to learn to anticipate the possibility of such occurrences, but once he has got to know his boat and how she can be expected to react, he should have very few handling problems indeed.

Most good cat designs can be controlled very precisely indeed, both as regards exact speed selection, and because they can literally be sailed right up to one's berth or mooring, and stopped at the very last moment. Thus the sometimes heart-stopping business of having to judge how far one's craft will shoot to windward, 'free-wheeling' with flogging canvas like the heavier keel-boats, is here cut to a matter of a very few yards or metres, so that handling in confined spaces becomes a really precise science.

By the same token, however, trying to sail too close to the wind, or pinching up through a narrow gap, are not things which many catamaran helmsmen will willingly attempt; so there are some manoeuvres which a multihull will simply not do under sail, yet which a clever monohull skipper will have no hesitation in trying. The chapter on handling, however, attempts to sort out these things in greater detail.

And few catamarans will tack satisfactorily under mainsail only, which some may consider a disadvantage.

JERKY MOTION

This same lightness has other effects. It adds some degree of comfort to a catamaran at sea. When driving hard to windward, she will not plunge down off the crests with quite that remorseless, seemingly inexorable 'crash-dive' one can experience in most keel-boats, when you begin to wonder how hard the seabed is going to be, or if the keel will fall off first and let you come up out of the trough again. The light-weight multihull will not crash down so heavily, but instead she will react to the wave surfaces more instantly and more accurately. The result, in rough going, can be an extremely rapid, jerky motion, which is to some extent less predictable than that of a keel-boat.

I have, however, classed 'Reduced Motion' as an advantage of the type. Partly because a cat does not roll as such, nor 'plunge' like a monohull, the violence of her motion is normally within perfectly tolerable limits, while the tiny angle of heel occasioned by sail pressures gives one's body one less aspect of movement to fight against.

In certain designs the bridgedeck is low, so as to keep down the Centre of Gravity and allow a sleek profile. Heavy slamming often results when close-hauled at speed. This *sounds* awful, but in a properly constructed cat will do little actual harm. Most modern designs however either have a pod (or 'nacelle') reducing the flat areas, or else have greater bridgedeck clearance, and do not pound.

EXCESS SPEED DANGERS

The available speed too, may have its disadvantages in severe conditions, in that it may, when beating or close-reaching, increase the 'arrival speed' of each sea under the boat, which in turn adds to the quick motion and strain on the rig. With the wind astern, motion is often barely perceptible, except for occasionally vivid acceleration and deceleration as she surfs or planes. And when luffing at speed, it has to be remembered that considerable centrifugal forces may be exerted, to add to the heeling movement of the wind.

It can therefore be not only wise, but kinder to both boat, gear, and crew to reduce sail early—very early—in an increasing wind, until a convenient compromise is made between forward progress and the superb comfort which catamarans are capable of giving, even when working hard to windward.

The big snag here is that the inherent lightness can provide insufficient momentum to help punch the boat to windward in a steep, short sea, *unless* she can at the same time be driven fairly hard.

52

CRITICAL SAIL AREAS

The correct amount of sail, then, for any given set of conditions *when beating* is far more critical in a catamaran than in a monohull.

Too much sail will quickly be seen and felt to be too much, yet much less than that might not be enough to drive her against heavy seas. A catamaran, after all, represents large bulk and windage above waterlevel, with very little 'grip' below it. In winds over Force 5, the top foot or so underneath the surface is often considerably aerated, which does nothing to help any shoal-draft boat, so she makes more leeway than something with a big deep keel stuck far down into the denser water.

When a gust hits a conventional, ballasted keel-boat, she first heels way over, spilling the initial forces up her sails. Gradually, as her momentum slowly builds up, she commences to increase her speed. Thus the weight of the wind is first totally wasted in heeling her, before she can start to drive more quickly forwards. The same applies, though to a *much* lesser extent, to trimarans.

A catamaran, on the other hand, because of her impressive 'initial' stability, does not heel when a squall strikes (unless she is *very* grossly overcanvassed indeed). All the drive of the wind is (has to be) converted at once into moving her forward in a rapid burst of acceleration, assuming of course that her sails were more or less correctly sheeted in the first place. This is why it can be argued that catamarans are more efficient sailing craft than conventional yachts; it is also why all sheets *must* be belayed *only* on quick-release 'jam' cleats or on some reliable automatic sheet-release gear. In the smaller cruising cat particularly, an excessive gust catching her with a large spread of canvas might well cause a hull to lift, and this is something which the prudent catamariner should *never* permit. (Sailing techniques in what one might call 'racing-dinghy' catamarans are quite another matter, but we are not discussing them.)

THE BUSINESS OF CAPSIZING

Any unballasted boat can be made to capsize, if you try hard enough, and it is this fact which worries most keel-boat enthusiasts about multihull sailing. In the average ballasted monohull you have a boat which, supposing her gear holds, can be knocked flat and will right herself either at once or in due course, so long as she has not filled. In most unballasted catamarans, you have a shape which is initially *extremely difficult* to heel over at all, let alone knock down. However, once this has actually happened, she may go right *on* over, unless something has been done to render total inversion impossible, such as masthead flotation. The question of capsizing is discussed in detail in Chapter 5.

However, I am a cruising man, and do not intend ever to sail my catamaran anywhere near her limits. Obviously, there comes the time in the course of coastal cruising particularly, when one is tempted to press on under over-much sail for a moment or two. (Squalls; nearly home-and-dry; that sort of thing.) But in those situations, when I know I'm pushing her, I sail the boat either with my own hand or someone else's on the sheets, ready to release them instantly should a hull show signs of trying to come unstuck. If there is still some distance to go, it is madness not to shorten sail—even if only to save the strain on the gear.

GOLDEN RULE

The Golden Rule for Multihull Sailing is simply this;

SHORTEN SAIL EARLY

Or, if you happen to prefer doggerel;

> 'Shorten sail *before* you must,
> Or risk capsize or something bust.'

That verse is nearly as awful as the threat it contains, but it's fun to chant as you go (or send somebody else) up forward to change jibs in worsening conditions.

Seriously, though; a very great deal can be done to prevent one's boat from ever nearing the risk of capsize, and indeed from actually inverting if she ever should be pushed too far. It is up to the individual owner to decide to have the gadgets or not, as he wishes. Capsizing happens as a result of one or several of only three things —bad seamanship, bad design, and *very* exceptional circumstances. I personally do not think that 'luck' has anything much to do with it.

HANDLING REQUIREMENTS IN BAD WEATHER

It is true to say that in very bad conditions at sea, most modern monohulled yachts will to some extent look after their crews.

It is equally true to say that in those same severe 'survival' conditions, most catamarans will probably require to be looked after by their crews—to some extent. But bear in mind how often you expect to be caught out in such conditions. Anyway, the compensation—a valid one, in my opinion—is that the crew of a catamaran is likely to be *far less* exhausted by bad weather than the crew of a monohull, whenever it does happen to them.

SPACE ON DECK

It has often been argued by keel-boat men (eyes wide in horror), that 'those huge open catamaran cockpits' must surely be a terrible danger at sea. They are, of course, almost always 'self-draining' cockpits, in that it is a very simple matter to have holes letting the water fall straight through into the gap between the hulls. In production catamarans, however, even I will admit that the holes provided are seldom big enough to handle the sort of volume of water which theoretically could come aboard—and frequently does come aboard *monohulls* in bad weather.

DISADVANTAGES BELOW DECKS

The space below decks must also be considered, for there are certainly one or two dangers there. For instance, all three of our children (catamariners since birth) have each, once, fallen down into a hull from the bridgedeck area. Similarly I regret to say, they have each, once, fallen down stairs at home. None of them has ever re-peated these experiments, nor have they been severely damaged when making either descent, thank goodness. But it *can* happen. Similarly, I have seen several minor injuries occasioned by people in socks slipping on the steps up from a hull to the bridgedeck saloon, in more than one cat. In our ship there is a rule that no one goes about in socks. Socks *and* shoes; or bare feet; but not socks only.

HEADROOM ON THE BRIDGEDECK

Also largely a matter of learning the hard way, is what happens occasionally when adults step up on to the bridgedeck from down under the full headroom in a hull. Most small catamarans have little more than sitting headroom in their centrally placed saloons. It has been suggested that bobble-caps or 'yottin keps' act as excellent sensors (*cat's* whiskers?) for the forgetful.

Trimaran and monohull sailors often criticise the lack of saloon headroom in many small catamarans, but it has to be remembered that in most cats the saloon is not a passage, as it is in other types of yacht, so by and large, one only sits there. So only sitting headroom is really required. The rule, when going below in those cats which have neither foot-wells in a 'pod' or 'nacelle' nor extra superstructure as in some Bill O'Brien designs, is '*Go in and sit down.*'

VISIBILITY FROM WITHOUT

The highly advantageous visibility from below decks afforded from the saloons and forecabins of most production catamarans (though by no means all) also means that anyone rowing past can similarly see pretty well *into* the bridgedeck area of the boat. Curtains may thus be considered a fairly necessary item of equipment, unless crews are highly extrovert exhibitionists.

BERTHING DUES

While the actual business of berthing alongside may be an easy matter for most catamarans, a fair number of Harbour Authorities see every chance of making larger profits, and charge *extra* dues for catamarans 'because they take up so much room'. Which is nonsense. I know of many quite normal motor-cruisers with a length similar to that of the two cruising cats I have owned, whose beam, when I asked, has turned out to be *within inches* of the beam of our own craft. Yet we have sometimes had to pay half as much again in harbour dues for the next-door berth, simply because our boat was one of those space-wasting catamaran things. Depending on where you sail this might or might not be much of a disadvantage, but it is one which I considider totally unfair and resent not a little. Most fishing boats working out of small ports will sport an overall beam of between fourteen and twenty-four feet. Beam for beam, catamarans are much shorter, so you can fit more of them alongside the same length of quay. Compared to other *yachts*, they are, length for length wider than monohulls, but not more than one third wider than the beamier ones. Even so, many authorities charge half as much again—which must be considered therefore as one of the disadvantages of the type, whether it is 'fair' or not.

MANOEUVRING PROBLEMS UNDER POWER

Another aspect of the berthing business, or rather that of entering harbour under power in anything of a blow with a steep sea running, occurs partly because of lightness and partly because of a light draft. In a strong headwind, with the fairly high windage of a light, high-riding catamaran, it may be difficult to retain control at low speeds, and furthermore, especially when a centreline outboard is hung on a bracket over the tail of the bridgedeck, propeller cavitation can sometimes by a serious problem. This is in part due to the fact that the 'inward' bow-waves tend, in choppy conditions, to be thrown together between the hulls, so that the water in which the propeller is trying to operate is full of bubbles, which a certain amount of pitching may do nothing to help. The only answer here is to ensure that the toe of the outboard is immersed as deeply as possible without swamping the engine.

FORE AND AFT MOTION—AND
THE 'SIDE WALLOP'

Pitching, indeed, is the one bit of motion to which catamarans are normally prone. They may not heel nor roll to any marked extent, but any hull with fine ends will pitch with great ease—'hobby-horsing', it is generally called. All catamarans have that tendency, but good design of bows and sterns can reduce it to a perfectly acceptable and normal level.

Also, if anything of a beam-on chop is running when sailing a catamaran in light airs, the inevitable side-to-side 'walloping' of such a boat and her rig, can completely shake what air there is right out of her sails, leaving her ignominiously standing while a lot of slow old monohulls go sliding smoothly by. One can avoid this only by altering course just enough to bring the seas off the beam—preferably on to the quarter.

So, basically, the principle disadvantages inherent in the catamaran concept are that while these boats can be made unsinkable, it is possible (with considerable difficulty) to persuade them to heel beyond the point of no return. They tend to require a more precise control of sail areas when beating, than do other types of craft. The motion, though less sick-making and less in extent than that of other yachts, is rapid and jerky. Control under power in strong winds may be difficult, and cavitation can be a considerable problem in boats not fitted with inboard engines. Catamarans may, in bad weather, need to be looked after by their crews, but are less exhausting to sail, so crews are normally more able to cope. But the next chapter looks more deeply into the whole business of sea-keeping in catamarans.

4

Sea-Keeping Catamarans

In the minds of many people the word 'catamaran' still conjures up instant thoughts of cranky, way-out craft with two hulls, which won't go to windward and will capsize anyway. All of which is no doubt due to past lack-of-knowledge errors on the part of those who built and those who sailed early cruising cats. We all make mistakes. Much press space in the 'Early Formative Years' of catamaran development was certainly devoted to the poor windward and capsizable qualities of the type.

For that reason, discussion of the sea-keeping abilities, and the reasons for the safety which many catamarans are capable of offering is, in my opinion, the most important part of this kind of book—and the next five chapters try to cover some of the ground in detail.

The term 'sea-keeping' generally means the ability to ride-out bad weather at sea, and to be able to keep on travelling in the desired direction for as long as possible, i.e. at least until the wind has attained gale force. (With any type of boat, it is normal for a large one to be able to sail on long after the smaller of its kind has hove-to, sought shelter, or is lying a-hull. So it is with catamarans.)

In other words, the quality of sea-keeping depends on how safe a given craft is in rough water—how well she handles, how 'sea-kindly' and therefore relatively comfortable she remains for her crew in heavy seas, and in the case of those frightful, freak 'monster' waves we give ourselves nightmares about and hope never to meet, how she may survive and whether or not she is likely to sink if things go drastically wrong.

It sounds like a chapter of horrors—but it isn't going to be. I have had no personal experience of such traumautic conditions, nor do I ever intend to have! But it behoves the Master of any ship, however small she might be, or however limited his cruising range is likely to be, to understand the mechanics, for want of a better word, of how a given design will be likely to react in bad conditions, should he ever find himself somehow faced with them, or anything like them.

BASIC CATAMARAN PRINCIPLES

So what, to begin with, makes a catamaran able to travel faster on occasions than a monohull? It is all to do with the well-established fact that a long narrow boat goes quicker than a long fat one. This is due to the wave-making propensities of the width when related to the length of any vessel disturbing that magic 'skin' dividing air from water. I am not going into the scientific explanations of waves and how they are formed—the fact that they happen is enough. But long, long ago, man discovered that while a canoe-like boat could be moved more easily and quickly than a chubbier craft, the chubbier craft tended to be better when he held up a kind of sail to catch the wind, if only because when a gust caught the chubby one sideways it tended to stay more upright, whereas the narrow canoe didn't.

It took the Polynesians to see that if you lashed, by means of outriggers (transverse spars), a second narrow hull or float parallel to the main hull but quite a distance from it, as opposed to right alongside, you retained the advantages of the long narrow boat's low wave-making (and so low-drag characteristic) ability to go fast easily. At the same time you had produced a more stable craft which could then be sailed, and sailed hard.

It was a film about Polynesia which around twenty years ago inspired two brothers, then builders of International Sailing Canoes and other dinghies, to go home and try lashing two of their racing products side-by-side and a bit apart, arrange something of a lash-up rig, and launch the result into the fawn-coloured waters of an Essex creek. The thing went like a rocket, was far too wet to be wise, and eventually began to break up before they returned, dripping and triumphant, with a gleam in their eyes which has since lit up the whole world of sailing. Roland and Francis Prout still lead the field of catamaran design today, always ready to learn more, try out new ideas, and invent singularly advanced craft with a combination of speed and safety characteristics which is apparently very hard to match.

The principle of the catamaran is simply that, then. Two easily moved, narrow hulls placed far enough apart to provide the necessary stability to hold up an efficiently large sail-plan. Theoretically, such a structure requires no ballast (which as any monohull sailor knows, is difficult to get moving, but which, once it *is* moving in a given direction, has considerable momentum to help it along). Having no heavy dead-weight in the form of ballast, a cat (or any multihull) can therefore exhibit a degree of acceleration hitherto unknown, and because of her narrow and shallow hulls, has so little friction that she is capable of very high speeds indeed in certain conditions.

SPEED

Let us look at this speed factor. A lot of hot air has wasted itself on the subject, and wondrous claims have

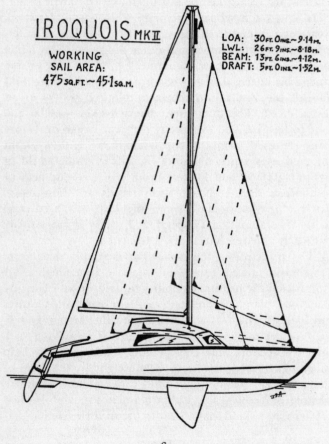

IROQUOIS MK II

WORKING
SAIL AREA:
475 SQ.FT. ~ 45·1 SQ.M.

LOA: 30 FT. 0 INS. ~ 9·14 M.
LWL: 26 FT. 9 INS. ~ 8·18 M.
BEAM: 13 FT. 6 INS. ~ 4·12 M.
DRAFT: 5 FT. 0 INS. ~ 1·52 M.

been made by many enthusiastic multihull owners. Whereas the highest potential speed (in knots) which a displacement monohull can maintain over long periods is calculable as about 1.4 times the square-root of her waterline length (in feet), catamarans have held between three and four times that speed, depending on their bulkiness. Thus a 25-foot W.L. monohull can sustain not much over seven knots, yet a cat the same length can, theoretically, top twenty-one knots.

But I am not here concerned with boats designed primarily for racing. While many cruising men do race,

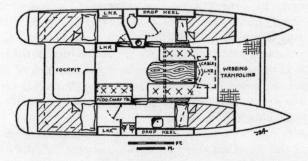

IROQUOIS Mk. II. Designed by J. R. Macalpine-Downie; sold by Sail Craft, Brightlingsea, Essex, England. Balsawood sandwich resinglass construction. Pivoting drop-keels and rudderblades; tiller steered with extensions allowing a variety of helming positions. Outboard motor, or with special extended sterns can be fitted with inboards. Luxurious mainly open-plan accommodation, sleeping 4 comfortably, 6/7 less so.

A very high performance Cruiser/Racer, obedient under sail, but requires careful handling when being sailed hard. Successor to the Mk. I. Smallest of range, others being 35-foot Cherokee, 40.8-foot Apache, and 46-foot Navaho.

most of us are more concerned with at least some degree of comfort and civilisation for our families and friends, and what interests us is how fast our boat is likely to go *on average* when cruising in the normal way. This is where catamarans can score very highly indeed. But notice that word 'can'.

In practice, when comparing the cruising speeds of monohulls and multihulls, it is only fair to take boats of similar designed purposes. Compare, if you like, an off-shore racing monohull of a given length with a similar-sized off-shore racing catamaran. Or take a comfortable, modern small cruising monohull of, say, nine metres length, as against a modern catamaran, designed for cruising, not racing, of the same length.

But let us stick to cruising. (When racing, too much depends on how good the crew are at hanging on till the last moment, and navigating to save the last inch of distance travelled through the water, to make actual boat comparisons anything like fair.) When simply cruising, we all have our moments of getting her going well, or pottering about under short canvas because it's a nasty day and we're not going far anyway, or even just drifting about in a calm because we aren't in a rush and the peaceful sunbathing is 'what we came for'.

So let's make our comparison of two similar-sized cruising boats, in the same waters, and over not just a passage or two nor even an entire cruise, but over the total entire cruises of a number of years, based on the *overall* average speeds of the two craft for time under way (sail *and* power) and distance travelled. Better still, these two craft were sailed by the same skipper. I have those figures, as it happens, because I have always kept detailed logs of all my cruising holidays, and can at a glance compare 'cruise average' speeds from year to year and craft to craft.

The two yachts in question are the 1959 8½-ton gaff cutter (converted to Bermudian ketch 1962) *Ocean Dove*, and the 1965 Prout Ranger 27 catamaran *Twintail*. Neither, in cruising trim, particularly fast boats.

Ocean Dove measured 28ft. 6in. stem to stern, and 24ft. 6in. on the waterline, with an overall beam of 9ft. 3in., working sail area 440 sq. ft., and auxiliary engine a 33hp diesel, giving 6 knots cruising.

Twintail measured 27ft. 3in. stem to stern, and 25ft. on the waterline, her overall beam being 12ft. 3in., working sail area 330 sq. ft., and auxiliary engine 20 hp Johnson outboard, giving 5 knots cruising.

The table below shows the results of four consecutive years of cruising in each boat, always from the same base in Strangford Lough, Northern Ireland, which is where I then lived. In each year shown, the boats crossed the North Channel over to the Firth of Clyde, went through the Crinan Canal and up the Scottish West Coast, and back again.

YEAR	YACHT	DISTANCE	CRUISE AVERAGE SPEED IN KNOTS	
1959	*Ocean Dove*	280 n.m.	@	3.3 kt.
1960	*Ocean Dove*	364 n.m.	@	3.9 kt.
1961	*Ocean Dove*	593 n.m.	@	3.4 kt.
1962	*Ocean Dove*	563 n.m.	@	3.4 kt.

Average distance: *450* n.m., and average speed: *3.5* knots.

YEAR	YACHT	DISTANCE	CRUISE AVERAGE SPEED IN KNOTS	
1967	*Twintail*	367 n.m.	@	4.2 kt.
1968	*Twintail*	525 n.m.	@	4.1 kt.
1969	*Twintail*	421 n.m.	@	4.1 kt.
1970	*Twintail*	428 n.m.	@	4.1 kt.

Average distance: *435* n.m., and average speed: *4.12* knots. (Speeds and distances *include* manoeuvring inside anchorages etc.)

It must be pointed out that the catamaran, *Twintail*, was on each cruise very low on her marks, because we found it necessary to carry considerably more weight on board than her designers designed her to carry. This was because we had three infants with us, and also I mostly needed a further adult to help crew the ship when Judy was dealing with the unending stream of 'emergencies'. *Twintail* was therefore never sailed anywhere near her potential maximum whereas *Ocean Dove* frequently was. We never, on any of our cruises in *Twintail*, saw the Sumlog read over ten knots, and rarely as much as seven. After we had sold her sadly, but to buy buy a bigger catamaran, her new owner had her bursting thirteen knots on her first North Channel crossing.

What *is* clear from the tables is that although the catamaran was so relatively heavily laden in comparison to the more 'beefy' conventional cruiser, and although her engine was less powerful (and more expensive to run), and although she carried noticeably less sail, particularly down-wind, her all-in average speed is just over half a knot *faster*. Carrying only normal weight on board she usually sailed on average a full knot or more faster than the monohull.

Even more interesting is the fact that our new catamaran, the 29ft. 3in. Catalac *Aku-Aku* whose waterline length is fractionally shorter than *Twintail*'s but whose beam is greater at 14 feet, when carrying just about the same weight and a little bit besides, is very much faster again.

Compare *Twintail*'s delivery trip from the Thames Estuary to County Down, *728 n.m. averaging 4.1 knots* in 1965, with *Aku-Aku*'s delivery trip (in uncannily similar weather conditions) from Christchurch Harbour, Hampshire, to the Kintyre Peninsula in Argyll, *706 n.m.*

averaging 4.9 knots in 1972. (We didn't hurry, in either case.) From this it seems that although she is undeniably more of a true cruising cat than the Ranger and her waterline length and sail area are similar to those of *Ocean Dove*, her average speed when cruising would seem to be more like 1½ knots faster than the conventional cruising yacht.

Two more interesting facts are that, as can be seen from the *Twintail* figures, catamarans tend to turn out a steadier average speed than monohulls, and secondly, as other figures I have shown very clearly, cats are (relative to monohull performances) slower racing boats than cruising boats.

If that sounds ridiculous, let me put it another way. If we were to race, say, *Ocean Dove* and *Aku-Aku* round the same triangular course in a given set of conditions (and ideally with the same crew!), there would quite probably not be anything like as great a difference between their finishing times as the above statistics would suggest. The difference will undoubtedly be there, but not maybe quite so glaringly obvious. And yet *Aku-Aku* is undoubtedly faster than *Ocean Dove* when cruising.

The reason for this is simply that *when racing* one is told where to sail, and you just get round the course as fast as you can. But when most of us go *cruising*, we tend to choose a course where possible which will give us the most pleasant sailing—'It's a fair wind for so-and-so today, let's go there for a change.' Everyone prefers not to have to beat when cruising, whether sailing monohull or multihull, and there is no doubt at all that across the wind or with it, most catamarans have the heels of otherwise comparable monohulls, and so are *noticeably faster when cruising*.

CAUTIOUS CATS

The safety of a cruising cat at sea again must depend to a great extent on people. People who designed her, people who built her, people who maintain her gear and equipment and hull, people who load her and fuel and provision her, and finally, the people who sail and navigate her. (They just *could* all be the same, I suppose!)

For the moment I will quite unfairly combine those who designed a given cat with those who built her. Let us say that they knew what they were about, of course, and saw to it that the construction and the shape were such as to provide all that her purchaser would be likely to expect of a boat of her Designed Purpose. And let us say, just for now, that she has been properly maintained, loaded, and all the rest of it, and that she is now at sea, and it's a bit rough. What then? The people. They are the factor which now makes her safe or unsafe—her crew.

CREW FATIGUE

A very readable paperback on the whole business of safety in yachts is '*The Small-Boat Skipper's Safety Book*' by Denny Desoutter (Hollis & Carter, 1972). He makes it quite clear that one of the greatest dangers lies in fatigue. The crew of any small boat out in a big sea can, and probably will, get tired very rapidly. The worse the motion, the more exhausted they become, partly because of a natural mental tenseness (which tightens muscles unnecessarily), but mainly because their bodies are automatically trying all the time to remain balanced in the face of very unbalancing forces. If sea-sickness sets in, things are made dozens of times worse. Even if it doesn't in some boats hot food may become out of the question, and tired bodies easily get cold and more exhausted than ever if not fed at least with something, and this encourages sea-sickness to start. And so on. And there we all are, in a state of quite remarkable inefficiency. And danger.

A tired navigator not only can make mistakes, but is likely to. A tired skipper (maybe the same person) is almost certain to make wrong decisions, even though one hopes these may be 'on the safe side', even when he could, perhaps, just have carried on and reached the original destination, rather than turning back.

So it stands to reason that if you can find some kind of a boat which tires her crew noticeably less than other types, she is, from the crew angle at least, going to be a safer boat. Fewer errors of judgement will be made in her than in a less sea-kindly craft; cooking will remain possible and the eating of the food more enjoyable far longer into oncoming bad weather. And her crew arrive at the end of a long passage brighter, and in a fitter frame of mind and maybe body too, to enter the new harbour or anchorage and cope with whatever decisions and problems they meet there, if any.

Let me quote again from *Children of Three Oceans* by Dr David Lewis, (Collins, 1969). The 45-foot catamaran *Rehu Moana* crewed by Dr and Mrs Lewis, their two small daughters and Miss P. Cairns, was on her homeward leg up the North Atlantic bound for England, when they were confronted by a severe gale, measured by instruments at 'Force 9 gusting 10', with a mean of fifty knots. *Huge* seas, as can be imagined all too easily.

Rehu Moana is broad-reaching under bare poles, towing all sorts of warps and chains and anchors astern.

71

Admittedly her crew *had* just completed a circumnavigation of the world, and so 'had their sea-legs', but all the same, the following remark by Dr Lewis is astonishing:

'With the whole gale at its height, Fiona cooked a lunch of chipped potatoes with fried bread and tomatoes, something that would have been impossible on a single-hulled vessel.' Whatever could I *possibly* add to that?

One might well argue that the act of frying (of all cooking methods, apparently 'deep frying' at that), was maybe not quite wise in a small yacht during a gale at sea, but that was surely a matter for the cook to judge at the time. The fact remains that it was not only possible to do so in a catamaran under those conditions, but also quite obviously successful as well from the consumers' point of view. And that says far more about how this type of vessel produces infinitely less motion at sea compared to 'normal' boats, than I can begin to say from my own personal experiences.

Be that as it may, in ten consecutive years of family cruising in much smaller catamarans than *Rehu Moana*, including many passages of sixty miles or so, my wife and daughters have never missed a meal at the cabin table through stress of weather—and we are not 'vacuum-flask-and-sandwich' people, fortunately. There have been no fiddles at the tables, either, and none of our cooking appliances has been gimballed—nor indeed were those on board Dr Lewis' big ocean-going cat.

Another useful attribute of the catamaran is that her living area is usually on the bridgedeck, and therefore makes a kind of sheltered forward extension of the cockpit, where the off-watch crew can keep warm and dry, and still be very much in touch with what is going on. Certainly, in those cats with low bridgedecks which tend to slam and bang to windward in heavy going, sleeping below decks is rendered difficult by the relatively high noise-level. But not all cats have that disadvantage nowadays. Good *rest* is anyway possible, even in the noisiest versions, because there is so little danger of being tipped out of one's bunk, as when a monohull heels to a squall.

MORE COMFORTABLE STEERING

Many modern cat designers are giving more thought to sheltering the helmsman, I'm glad to say. (I mostly cruise in Hebridean waters, where even on an otherwise 'hot' day, the winds can be bitterly cold.) Once again this cuts down on fatigue, for shivering can be very tiring!

A further aspect of this fatigue business is the fact that for some reason sitting at the helm of a catamaran (particularly if she is wheel-steered) is noticeably less tiring than the same job in a monohull. I have frequently done ten and twelve hour tricks, when I know for a fact that four would have been more than enough in the same conditions in a monohull.

So, the crew of a catamaran at sea has a *much* easier time of it than the crew of a monohull. And that for a start makes the whole business of putting to sea not just safer by a considerable margin, but a lot less worrying for the skipper.

5

Capsizes Cut Down to Size

The possibility of a capsize is the one thing which worries most monohull skippers, who might otherwise be attracted to cats. I can assure them without any hesitation that there is *no need to worry*. At least, they need worry only about themselves, because if a cruising cat should ever capsize, it will be the skipper's fault, just as it would if he ran his ship on a rock ...

After all, in driving a car, one endeavours not to turn it over on a corner. So it is when sailing a catamaran. It really is quite difficult to get one to capsize—and there is no *need* to do such a thing! In fact, the whole answer to the 'capsize problem' is very simple.

Don't!

THE IMPORTANCE OF DESIGN

Not *all* cats are completely perfect from the safety point of view. Some are, after all, designed mainly with speed in mind, and to attain the best performance in any kind of craft, certain other things have to be foregone. Clearly a lot of canvas on a pair of extremely fine hulls will go faster than less canvas set above wider, more buoyant hulls. Amongst British designs, these two extremes are represented by the very sporty Macalpine-Downie designs which can go wickedly fast when pushed (and still make quite good cruisers of course), and the Bill O'Brien concept which is virtually uncapsizeable but naturally nothing like as thrilling to sail.

All through this book I find myself stressing that one should choose not just *any* catamaran when thinking of getting such a boat, but a catamaran designed particularly to suit the type of sailing one intends to do in her.

At the moment, between the designers mentioned above, comes a pretty adequate range of craft which attempt to strike some balance between speed and security. I am not suggesting for a moment that any of Rod Macalpine-Downie's excellent catamarans are dangerous, for not only would any such suggestion be utterly libellous, but totally wrong and misleading! Like any true thoroughbred, a catamaran from his drawing board is likely to require careful, skilful handling when she is being sailed *hard*—but she will then provide mile upon mile of fast, comfortable cruising. Or racing. What I *am* saying is simply what the facts have shown.

The Bill O'Brien Bobcat—a boat designed primarily with safe family cruising in mind—has, as far as I can determine, no record of capsizes, whereas the far more racey Macalpine-Downie Iroquois Mks I & II cats have not that boast to their credit. Let me stress that I know of no capsizes of Macalpine-Downie designs which were attributable entirely to factors outside the control of their crews.

This, generally speaking, amounts to saying that the faster catamarans can be over-driven to a danger-point, more readily than the slower ones. For all that, the shapes of the *ends* of the hulls have a good deal to do with the 'safeness' of either type, whether she is a slim flyer or a more homely, 'motherly' cruiser.

75

THE SHAPE THAT COUNTS

Shape, both of hulls and rig, is really the crux of the whole matter. Not the sizes, so much as the shapes of these two things decide how easy or difficult it is going to be to capsize a given cruising cat. And the variety of shapes, even amongst the relatively small number of cat designs available at the time of writing, is surprising.

There is everything from the 'half Vee' cross-section of asymmetrical hulls, to the 'full Vee' (either narrow- or wide-angled), with and without chines. There are 'V' hulls which are very nearly 'U' hulls, and 'U'-shaped hull sections practically carried from stem to stern, and others again which are 'Veed' for about half their length, gradually changing to pretty flat 'U' sections aft.

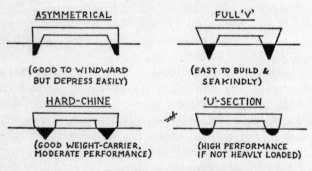

ASYMMETRICAL
(GOOD TO WINDWARD BUT DEPRESS EASILY)

FULL 'V'
(EASY TO BUILD & SEAKINDLY)

HARD-CHINE
(GOOD WEIGHT-CARRIER, MODERATE PERFORMANCE)

'U'-SECTION
(HIGH PERFORMANCE IF NOT HEAVILY LOADED)

BASIC HULL SHAPES

There are fine bows to cut through waves at speed; chine bows which are fuller and won't; rounded profiles; angular profiles; clipper profiles. There are transom sterns designed for high performance in a breeze; fine tapered sterns for least resistance in light airs; sterns

which provide lots of reserve buoyancy; others which
theoretically 'balance' the bows. And, as I have already
said, there are hulls with narrow waterline-dimensions,
and hulls with wide waterline-dimensions, quite apart
from topsides which flare outwards; others which curve
up and inwards, and those which go straight up and
stop, resulting in a box-like appearance and rude comments.

It would be quite ridiculous to say that this or that
shape (or combination of shapes) is best, because, just
as in monohull design, what is best for racing is not
usually best for cruising, and even what is good for one
kind of cruising will be far short of ideal for another.

(I haven't mentioned the wide range of 'keels' which
the various catamarans produced today have, or have
not. But I will.)

THE CHOICE...

What one has to decide, when choosing a boat, is what
sort of sailing you want her for—and *then* decide what
shape of hull and type of rig is going to be the most
suitable. To do that, it is as well to know a little of what
effect the various shapes have on performance; which
term I take to mean safety at sea as well as speed, comfort, and all the rest of it.

...AND WHAT GOES WRONG

Catamarans have what has been rather well described as
'straddle stability'. That is to say their basic stability
against heeling moments of the rig rely on her having
two parallel floats or hulls, held securely apart at a given
distance (the usual overall beam being between 0.4 and

0.5 times the overall length). This forms, in effect, a pretty 'untippable' platform. However, if the floats are very fine and narrow, they can individually be pushed down into the water more easily than if they were each broad and buoyant. If they are *too* broad and buoyant, of course, they become individually like narrowish monohulls lashed side-by-side, and the massive wave-making overcomes the ability to sail fast. That is the designer's problem!

So, taking the two hulls, and putting mast and sails above them, and a wind blowing from one side; what happens? If the gust is not strong enough initially to make her lift a hull at once and so start to capsize, theoretically the aerodynamic forces of the sails act, and the boat begins to accelerate. But before *that* happens, the wind forces, which are thus directed by the sails into the equivalent of a thrust pointing roughly over the lee bow of the boat, try to pull the rig in *that* direction. And since the rig is firmly attached to the boat by shrouds, backstays and so on, this thrust is converted instantly downwards, depressing the lee bow—or trying to.

Here is the point. If the bows of the craft are fine and knife-like, there is very little to stop them biting deeply into the water. The underwater parts of a catamaran's hulls are usually long, shallow, and pretty flat, when seen from the side. And it is that side profile which is being presented to the water by what I will call the 'leeway' force of the sails. All that stops the cat sliding sideways is her shallow profile and whatever drop-keels or other means she has of counteracting leeway.

Now, when one bow is first tipped down, there is momentary drag on that side of the centreline. If it is the lee bow, you get noticeable lee helm. But it *is* only

for a moment, for at once a more powerful force charges
into play. When a bow leading such a long and shallow
hull is depressed, relative to its stern, the centre of the
area offered sideways on to the water (known as the
Centre of Lateral Resistance, or CLR) obviously moves
right away forwards of its normal position. This does two
things. It destroys the delicate balance of the sail-plan in
relation to the hull, which tends to swing the stern round
and force the boat up into the wind; and at the same
time, because the bow has suddenly more grip of the
water than the stern, the stern is much more able to slide
round as directed by the now unbalanced rig, than it was
when the craft rode level. So one now has a quite extraordinary tendency for the boat to luff round out of
control.

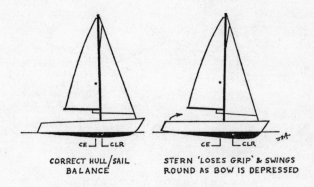

CORRECT HULL/SAIL
BALANCE

STERN 'LOSES GRIP' & SWINGS
ROUND AS BOW IS DEPRESSED

A DIFFERENT TECHNIQUE

Now, most single-hulled sailors would say: 'Well, good!
She is luffing automatically, and will therefore be all
right.' True, when a monohulled keel-boat gets over-
powered in a squall you *do* luff her, to spill wind from

her sails and ease her upright again. But *you should not do this in a multihull.*

Centrifugal force; that's why! If a catamaran has lifted a hull clear of the water (to look at an extreme case again), she is very delicately balanced indeed in a lateral sense, as anyone can see. If you now try to turn her in such a direction as will add anything at all to that centrifugal thrust (in other words if you let her luff up into the wind at speed), long before she releases enough pressure out of her sails, her own weight, the weight of her rig and so on, all combine to push her quickly over —beyond that delicately hung 'point of no return'. Many racing dinghy helmsmen will know just what I mean!

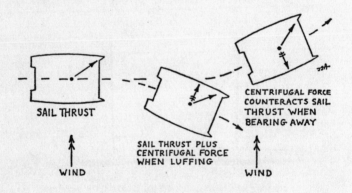

SAIL THRUST

WIND

SAIL THRUST PLUS
CENTRIFUGAL FORCE
WHEN LUFFING

CENTRIFUGAL FORCE
COUNTERACTS SAIL
THRUST WHEN
BEARING AWAY

WIND

RUDDERPOST ANGLES

There is a far more important factor. If a catamaran has her rudders hung on those fashionable 'trailing transoms'—the kind whose top edge is further forward in the boat than their lower edges, it doesn't take much imagination to see that when the blade is put over hard at speed, it generates quite a lot of *lift*. This not only vastly reduces the effectiveness of the blade (like the heeled over sails of a monohull), it also helps to lift the already lifted stern of the boat, which again reduces rudder effect and *helps to dig the bow in*, adding seriously to the generally unbalanced condition of the whole ship.

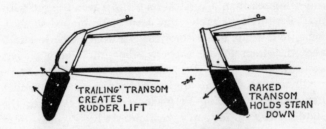

'TRAILING' TRANSOM CREATES RUDDER LIFT

RAKED TRANSOM HOLDS STERN DOWN

FOIL EFFECT OF RUDDER-POST ANGLE WHEN HELM IS APPLIED AT SPEED

To put all *that* in a nutshell is to say that the less skilled the crew, the more vertical should be the catamaran's rudders—vertical, or preferably even angled the other way, on a raked-*back* transom whose top is well abaft its lowest point—like that of a Folkboat monohull, for example. Then if the helm has to be put over at speed, instead of it lifting the stern, the rudder tends to bite down into denser water, giving better performance and helping to some extent, however small, to counteract the depression of the boat's bow.

A vertically hung rudder is probably the best compromise, though usually not necessarily the most aesthetic answer, unless considerable architectural skill is applied. John Winterbotham, who designed the hull of the Catalac, got over the vertical transom eye-sore by extending 'false' topsides which end in a pleasing rake aft beyond the edge of the transoms themselves, and the

Prout Snowgoose 34 does it very smartly with canoe-type sterns faired into the rudders, which then have their own 'tail-end' profiles.

But this is all part of looking for the right features for the sort of sailing *you* want to do. Many designers will maintain that a 'trailing transom' is more buoyant in a following sea than a vertical one, and I won't argue with that. Personally, I prefer the stern to be shaped so as to make it difficult for a following sea or its crest to climb aboard, which to me suggests something more or less vertical.

Obviously, a *slight* angle either way on the rudder hanging is not going to make *much* difference to the rudder effect, so long as it is slight. At high speed, water becomes in effect so dense and powerful that it can have astonishingly exaggerated results in its efforts to make an easier route round obstructions such as hard-over rudders. But for all that, even if rudders *are* hinged at the worst possible angles, they are *not* the reason that catamarans can and have capsized.

ABOUT CAPSIZES

Any 'accident'—any capsize—is almost always a matter of not just one or two factors taking place, but several things all combining and coinciding at just the wrong moment (human error not the least).

There is no more need to sail a catamaran so near her limits that capsize is even *remotely* likely, than there is to sail one of those highly popular (and a hundred-times more capsizable) racing dinghy class boats near *her* limits when you have the family and friends on board for an afternoon sail. Thus, even the so-called 'cruising' cat which has in fact been designed with high racing performance in mind, can be cruised perfectly safely, so long as her crew are prepared *not to drive her* up towards her full potential on any course. It's like having a powerful, thoroughbred sports car—you don't *have* to drive it flat out all the time—especially when there are those on board who might be 'put off' if sufficiently frightened or injured. The most unlikely craft *imaginable* have crossed the Atlantic Ocean safely—and a lot of well-designed and well-built ones haven't!

ACTUAL INCIDENTS

Capsizes have happened when sometimes the state of the seas running at the time had considerable bearing on the matter—but not always. If we have to go into the nasty details (and what better way to learn), one capsize which most catamaran folk heard about was the *Golden Cockerel* inversion in the lee of the Isle of Wight, during a race. (And her poor owner, who has *since* sailed many thousands of ocean miles in her, must be very tired indeed of reading what other people, who weren't there, have to say about it. So I hope he'll forgive me.)

Golden Cockerel was being slightly over-sailed during the Crystal Trophy Race—over-sailed, in the sense that many people push their boats to the very edge of their limits when racing. Fair enough. We all know that you *can* sail a catamaran with only one hull in the water, and get away with it. It is normal procedure in 'racing dinghy' catamarans. And *Golden Cockerel* and other cats there got away with it several times, that day.

Very fresh wind, and several comparably sized cats going equally well in the close vicinity. Some were fitted with automatic sheet-release gears, and I have heard it rumoured that these 'tripped out' so frequently in the squalls coming off the high Island shore, as to be a nuisance. In the relatively still water in the lee of the land, these gadgets were set at too small an angle of heel to let the boats concerned get anywhere near their Points of No Return. The settings would be right at sea later on, but not just then, and it seems that the things had been locked or by-passed by some of the crews. In the big *Golden Cockerel*, however, they were having a wonderful sail, and crewmen were no doubt ready to cast off the sheets by hand should it become necessary. It became necessary, but the genoa sheet jammed and would not release, and by the time other things were tried it was too late anyway.

What I want to stress here is that it was not just the large sail area and the jammed sheets that mattered at that moment of truth—it was the hull shape as well. Once well heeled (difficult though that may be to achieve) many catamaran designs will begin to slip sideways, because their hull shape allows this to happen, and this naturally releases some of the tripping effect of the water, by letting it slide away underneath the hull.

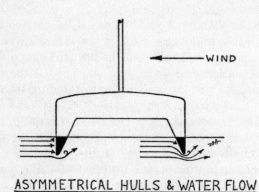

ASYMMETRICAL HULLS & WATER FLOW

Golden Cockerel had what are known as asymmetrical hulls. That is, the outboard side of, for instance, the port hull is almost vertical, while the inboard side of it is flared, representing a narrow 'V' in section which is canted over so that one leg of the 'V' is upright. The starboard hull being similarly canted the other way, no matter which tack the boat is on, the lee side of her is virtually an upright wall, so to speak; a shape which is highly resistant to leeway, especially when some kind of drop-keel is added to each hull in an appropriate position. This particular hull-form is therefore excellent for racing, where windward work is all-important.

But, with the bottom of each 'V' being outboard, as it were, once the boat heels, she will still have a lot of resistance to sideways slip. Furthermore, such narrow hulls as these—particularly at the bows where so much pressure is brought to bear down from the rig above—can be relatively easily pushed deeply into the water if the weight is not taken equally by both of them. Which lessens the chance of side-slip even more! The jammed sheet of that big genoa was in *Golden Cockerel* the final straw when she was already flying a hull, and over she went.

Again, in what I believe to be the only case of a Prout Ranger capsizing in anger, one of the several critical factors just may have had a little to do with the design of the forward part of the yacht. Not the prime fault, but as ever, just one of many things which came together at the wrong moment.

Haxted Argo II, as she was called, went over in the mouth of the River Elbe. The trouble here was a considerable gale of wind, before which she was running, quite comfortably and safely, under a tiny storm jib (so tiny that no one could possibly suggest she was 'blown over' by it). All was well enough, apart from it being a horrid day.

Her owner knew that if he arrived at all soon off the great river mouth, the ebb would still be running and the seas might be bad. However, they were not hurrying, and all his pilot information showed that by the moment they got to the worst place, the stream should be well slackened, and any overfalls would be minimal. Heavy rain in the mountains earlier that week, or what, nobody knows—there was a great deal more tide sluicing out smack into the gale when *Haxted Argo* came foaming in than there should have been.

Three gigantic, freak waves formed. *Enormous* ones. The catamaran—a 31-foot version of the famous Ranger 27—tobogganed down the first two; slowed, and let them pass ahead under her without trouble. But the third was altogether too steep. *Haxted Argo* II went whizzing down the face of that third sea at a quite fantastic angle. When she hit the bottom of the trough her fine bows stuck right in—some of her crew were hurt by being flung against the cabin bulkhead. The sea came on, and she was more or less cartwheeled, in a similar manner to the famous *Tsu Hang* incident (a large monohulled ketch which 'planed' down a vast sea in the Roaring Forties, dug her bow in and virtually went end-over-end). *Tsu Hang* almost filled, and equally almost sank.

Haxted Argo shipped vast amounts of water through her open companion hatch, but did not sink. She was, however, fitted with masthead buoyancy, and so floated —for about four minutes probably—on her port side, during which the crew had time to launch the liferaft and put necessities into it. Then she righted herself. (*Golden Cockerel* had no such flotation, and she turned right upside down. In neither case was anyone drowned.)

Haxted Argo could then have been bailed out and sailed on, and indeed would have been, had not a very worried coaster captain seen the incident and pretty well insisted on 'rescuing' her crew, mangling and chopping the poor catamaran to pieces with his ship's propeller in the process. This was very much in the early days of cruising catamarans, and he had obviously seen what he took to be a maritime disaster; a small yacht which although it had not sunk, clearly (he thought) would soon do so. He did what he thought best, and the catamaran's crew, suffering no doubt from shock at that moment, and being unable to manoeuvre their now sluggish craft out of his way under such a scrap of sail, had no alternative but to accept his 'assistance'.

It is well worthy of note that *Haxted Argo*'s owner replaced her at once with another catamaran. His opinion is that none of the monohulls he had previously cruised in could possibly have survived *any* of those three freak seas—and would hardly have given their crews time to get out, let alone mess around with flares and things, and launch and provision liferafts ...

How delightfully easy it is to be wise after any event! But at the time of the *Haxted Argo II* incident, I happened to own a Ranger myself, a 27-footer which varied from her only in having four feet less boat abaft the cockpit. And naturally I wanted to know exactly *why* *Haxted Argo* had tried to nose-drive, or at least why she had tripped herself up by digging her bows under. Her minute storm jib could hardly have contributed, though conceivably it may have added a small amount to her speed as she came sledging down the face of that sea. It certainly could not of itself have capsized her, since, for one thing, the wind was dead aft.

It is clear from her owner's invaluable and highly detailed account of what happened, a copy of which he very kindly gave me, that the boat simply shot downhill and hit the bottom of the steep trough at high speed. The Ranger's bows are of the 'knife-edge' variety; fine practically all the way up to deck level. These of themselves have hardly any reserve buoyancy, and so can knife-in pretty readily. Now, in the ordinary course of sailing, this matters very little in this particular design, because the Prouts had given her the right sort of bridgedeck shape to go with them. It was very strongly constructed, and so shaped and positioned that if the boat pitched heavily, or tried to 'run-in' in any ordinary sea condition, the bridgedeck would 'bottom' forward, banging down on the water to provide instantly a most arresting amount of reserve buoyancy. If heavily laden, this of course may produce a good deal of slamming and banging when going to windward hard, but otherwise is no great disadvantage. It is, in fact, an advantage, in preventing almost any attempt to nose-dive from becoming even remotely dangerous.

Unfortunately the sea in the gale-torn mouth of the River Elbe that fateful day was not just 'any' sea—it was a very specific, very freak sea indeed. It seems that *Haxted Argo*'s bridgedeck entered the water at an incredibly steep angle—solid water actually rose up the cabintop and entered the hulls via the large companion hatch, which had slid open under the impact and weight of a crewman who was flung against it. For the all-important second or two while the wave followed her up, she was stuck there with all momentum arrested, so not unnaturally she fell over, and lay with her streamlined masthead float fully justifying its existence while her crew sorted themselves out.

ANTI-CAPSIZE FEATURES

It is my belief that another catamaran of similar size, but first with even a 'knuckle' chine to provide *a lot* more reserve buoyancy low in the bow of each float, plus *considerably more freeboard*, might have avoided the digging-in to the same extent, and so might have avoided capsizing before the same sea. The next boat the Prout brothers designed does in fact have a lot more buoyancy forward.

All is compromise, though. If too much buoyancy is provided right forward in the bows, the boat will be very slow—through trying to burst her bulky 'entry' through that surprisingly tough air/water 'skin' which dogs all surface craft. So far as I am aware, no one has yet tried building a catamaran with the sort of bulbous underwater protuberances one sees on the bows of modern cargo ships. Granted, this would hardly be classed as 'reserve' buoyancy, since it would normally be totally immersed, but the fact that it enabled a craft to have a basically buoyant end to start off with, might have most interesting effects.

In any event, in the case of *Haxted Argo* we have a catamaran capsizing without being 'blown over'. Automatic sheet-release gear would not have helped. It is well known that Prout Rangers had (for they are no longer being built) less than average beam. Perhaps more beam might have prevented her losing her balance when up-ended, though I doubt it unless this were coupled with better bows, etc. What saved her (if for this purpose we discount the fact that the coaster later destroyed her) was her masthead float. So, let's take a look at masthead floats in general.

MASTHEAD BUOYANCY

There are two schools of thought here. One says you ought to have a masthead float because if you ever *should* capsize it will prevent the cat from turning right upside-down, which is theoretically true. One says you shouldn't have them, because if you sail the boat sensibly she should never get anywhere *near* capsize point without one, but with one the weight and the windage of such an object right at the top of the mast is bound considerably to increase the risk of capsizing, which is also theoretically true. So what *is* best? Again, what sort of sailing are you likely to do in your particular catamaran, and which of these two arguments do you as an individual feel is the most valid?

If you start off with a design which is basically not very likely to capsize in the first place, then there is little need to bring actual capsize-point nearer by having the risks imposed by the weight or windage of a float aloft. If, on the other hand, you have chosen a design which might be every bit as stable when at rest, but which becomes more easily capsized through over-driving (due to hull shape, rig, or whatever), then it is only sense to put up with adequate and appropriate equipment, whatever the snags may be, simply because the 'off-chance' may not be quite so far away. (And if a cat is to be raced anyway seriously, I would *definitely* fit her with an m/h float.)

Suppose then, for whatever reason, we have decided to have a masthead float—what sorts are there, and which seem best? One has only the records, such as they are, for a guide.

FIXED FLOATS

One of the most commonly seen (because it has frequently been fitted to several well-known designs) is the 'flying saucer' shape of float—something like an athlete's discus, or two large saucers stuck together edge-to-edge and mounted flat over the top of the mast. The advantage of this kind is that it offers minimal windage whether the craft is at moorings or sailing to windward or on any other course. The disadvantage, and it is a serious one, is that more than one of these has broken off when actually put to the test on a capsized boat's mast.

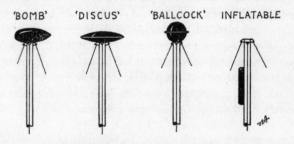

'BOMB'   'DISCUS'   'BALLCOCK'   INFLATABLE

SOME TYPES OF MASTHEAD FLOAT

For some unfortunate reason, when a catamaran is capsized, she tends to blow downwind *masthead foremost*. One would think that since the hull has obviously more windage than anything else when she is lying on her side, she would gradually swing round until her masthead was upwind, which would then help her to right herself; but this is *not* the case. The drag of the side-decking and so forth seems to overcome the thrust of the windage on the hull and bridgedeck, sufficiently to prevent her moving any other way but mast foremost. And

91

the 'flying saucer' type of float is then presented flatways on to the sea, and at surprising speed.

Another sort of fixed float is the 'bomb' shape—a fat, torpedo-like thing. This shape is fine when the craft is head-to-wind at her anchor, and very effective indeed in the water, where it provides plenty of lift and not much drag. The trouble is that when beating or reaching the windage of such a shape, fixed fore-and-aft at the mast-head, is considerable, and could, one would then suppose, contribute something to a flip. This was the sort of float common to early Ranger catamarans, *Haxted Argo II* and my own *Twintail* included.

Michael Henderson, catamaran designer and ingenious inventor, got over this on one of his boats by placing a 'bomb'-type float on a swivel, and giving it very weapon-like fins at the narrow, tail end. Thus it acted as a wind-vane *and* minimised the windage by remaining perpetu-ally streamlined automatically. It also sorted out the smaller snag presented by other fixed floats which can make it hard to see the burgee from the helm! Hender-son's swivel-float tended to oscillate in a fresh breeze though, so how good it was as a wind indicator, I couldn't say.

A third type, to be seen on the recent Bill O'Brien Channel Rover, Amazon, and associated designs, is what I can only describe as the 'ball-cock' shape (literally, a spherical object with a joint line round its equator). And from an all-round windage point of view, when speaking of fixed 'solid' floats, this has to be the best when you consider how good it will be in the water as well—what-ever it actually *looks* like! With typical O'Brien cunning, on his boats they incorporate a small radar reflector, though since this all weighs in the region of 28 lb., I am not too sure how good a thing that is.

BALLOON FLOATS

Then there are several kinds of gas-filled balloon mast-head floats. These have the advantage of having no windage problems when not in actual use, and they are fairly light as well. Some are automatically gas filled by a carefully designed mechanical switch activated by an ex-. cessive angle of heel; some are manually triggered; and some operate when they find themselves wet with sea-water.

Aesthetically, apart from the windage thing, these are better than 'solid' m/h buoyancy, but there is always that little question at the back of one's mind, especially after several seasons of the thing never having been operated; namely, 'if it comes to the crunch, will it work as it should?' At least one I know of *has* failed to inflate fully, so there is that chance, however remote it might be. I also know of one which inflated right enough when the boat went over, only to burst at once, with inevitable sadness all round.

I tend naturally to be wary of 'gadgets', so where I think a masthead float is at all likely to be needed, I would prefer to have a fixed thing that was always at the ready, without anything mechanical, chemical, or electrical being needed to make it work. All these gears are of course kept as simple and fool-proof as their manufacturers can make them, and there is very little that can go wrong with any of them.

BALLASTED KEELS

The whole business of ballast keels in catamarans has been long discussed and tried. Mike Henderson was, I think, the first to try the 'belt and braces' system on his *Golden Miller*, way back in 1958. She was a small catamaran with 'U'-sectioned hulls, each of which had a deep fin keel with ballast, just like that of a conventional yacht. She also had a 'flying saucer' masthead float, and, having passed the test-model stage adequately in the Henderson household's bathroom, the real thing was built. Before invited cameras, the finished yacht was sailed out on the Solent one very windy day, to see what would happen.

She behaved most spectacularly. Carrying *far* more sail than was reasonable (or sensible) for the conditions, for test purposes, Henderson repeatedly flattened her over in the squalls until she was far beyond any unballasted catamaran's Point of No Return—and she always rose up again and sailed on. Which must in itself have been very satisfying.

The trouble with putting ballast, as such, into a catamaran is that you at once drastically reduce one of the type's main advantages —that of ultra light displacement. The heavier she is, the more the wave-making, and the slower the speed. But there is another problem associated with this kind of craft. When she does get up speed, on a reach for example, in anything of a sea the strains on her underwater surfaces become considerable, and things like dagger-boards or keels, rudder-blades too, suffer heavy buffeting effects.

I was one day sailing a Shearwater III racing cat (my second) in a race on Belfast Lough. There was a brisk breeze, and the course after the start took us away on a beam reach. That particular Shearwater was fitted with shortish, twin dagger-boards, and because making the start had involved windward work, these were fully down. We rocketed away, sheets still hard in as was necessary for reaching at really high speed in that wind. In seconds we were doing maybe sixteen knots, when there was a bang and the lee stern cocked itself up completely clear of the water. The *lee* stern?

Looking over, I discovered that one of the thick marine-ply dagger-boards had sheared off where it left the hull, shot aft, and been impaled on the leading edge of the alloy rudder-blade. The two had met edge-to edge at right-angles, and the alloy had cut deep into the wood, the front edge of which had risen at once under the force of water, and was now acting as a most efficient hydrofoil, *lifting* the stern of the boat.

The point here is first to emphasise the fierceness of the strains which are imposed on keels of any kind by catamarans travelling at speed, and secondly to say that keels which have blobs of ballast at their feet would seem to be even worse off than those which don't. *Misty Miller*, a larger development of Mike Henderson's earlier *Golden Miller*, lost a ballast keel in the 1964 Observer Single-Handed Transatlantic Race (OSTAR for short), wrenched off at its roots. Her intrepid owner retired, but managed to sail a badly leaking boat to the Azores, where he decided that while carrying out repairs, both keels might be made safer *without* the ballast, and had all of it removed.

Rehu Moana, the first catamaran to sail round the world, also had one of her original ballasted drop-keels break off and depart unexpectedly, and in much the same way. David Lewis also decided that she would be better without ballast, and that anyway there was no need for it, with the great straddle-stability of his catamaran. He appears to have been right, too, for more than once after that, the boat was caught with far too much sail up in gale-force squalls, and nothing upsetting happened. Dr

Lewis then experimented with wooden dagger-boards in various positions, but because his boat was carrying a rig that wasn't designed for her, she also carried a great deal of weather helm. The dagger-boards too broke off repeatedly, showing once more the forces that can be imposed by a boat which refuses to heel and either spill air off the tops of her sails or spill water under her keels.

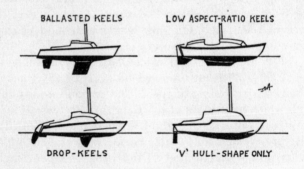

BALLASTED KEELS   LOW ASPECT-RATIO KEELS

DROP-KEELS   'V' HULL-SHAPE ONLY

UNDERWATER PROFILES

It seemed to Dr Lewis that an answer might be long, low-aspect-ratio keels fixed permanently along the bottom of the hulls. Because of the weather helm, he had these made so that they tapered from nothing forward until they were at their deepest right aft, and this made a definite improvement.

At about the same time, the Prout brothers were experimenting with long shallow fixed keels for their Ranger catamarans. There is a lot of theory behind this, as well as certain factors which affected the Ranger class alone. Basically though, it had been found that in a choppy sea, it was sometimes hard to drive a Ranger fast enough to windward to prevent her pivoted drop-keels (with which the early boats were fitted) from stalling, and letting the boat make excessive leeway. It was thought that perhaps long 'old-fashioned' shallow keels would stall less easily, and indeed this proved to be so, for later on I fitted my own *Twintail* with a pair of these shallow keels, and removed her drop-keels and their naturally heavy cases completely.

The result was remarkable. Admittedly we as a family always sailed *Twintail* in a very over-loaded state, and coupled with that, I never liked to carry a lot of sail when our tiny daughters were on board. So far we had managed to avoid frightening them with anything that happened when we were sailing, and so never pressed the boat deliberately. (It of course occasionally happened accidentally that we got caught in an unexpected increase of wind, but we had plenty in reserve before the boat became frantically over-pressed. That way I always had time in hand to make suitable sail reductions before shouting panic set in!)

Often and again with the drop-keels, we had made slow passages to windward, but as soon as the fixed, low-aspect-ratio keels were fitted, her windward performance in a seaway improved out of all recognition, although she was still pretty slow compared to less deeply laden Rangers. But now she could forge ahead even under a scrap of canvas, making very little leeway. The long keels had an impressively low stalling speed, and handling was impaired only by her increased turning-circle; otherwise it was much enhanced, and she was far more sure-footed when tacking.

There is, however, a further consideration, since we are talking of keels, which is also bound up with the business of capsizing (or *not* capsizing, I should say).

Quite obviously, a deep keel sticking down below a catamaran, whether she is being pressed sideways by wind or
by wave, will tend to catch, as it were, in the denser
water beneath her, and act as a tripping device. Which
nobody wants. In the case of a drop-keel or keels of
course, it is possible—and *right* when riding out bad
weather—to raise at least partially one or both boards,
so that the boat *can* slip sideways easily. The trouble
is, while still maybe desperately trying to make head-
way to windward, one is most unlikely to do anything
which might increase leeway, and one is tempted to
leave both boards down and is thus left with the tripping
risk.

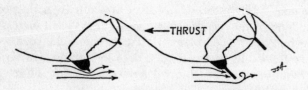

'SLIPABILITY' OF LOW ASPECT-RATIO
KEELS AS COMPARED WITH DEEPER ONES

If a catamaran has been built with *fixed* keels, it is
not possible to do anything to reduce the tripping effect
when she is thrust sideways. This suggests very strongly
that the deep fin type of keel is not a particularly safe
thing to have under a catamaran. The shallow, low-
aspect-ratio keel (pair of keels, that is) is another matter.
Mostly, they are fitted to round-bilged hull-forms ('U'
sectioned hulls, in other words). Whenever the hull is
severely heeled, part of the belly of that 'U' comes between the flow of water across the bottom of the boat
and the keel, so that the keel's effect is much reduced,

letting the boat slide safely away sideways and 'ride the punch'.

You may well say 'Dear help us, I hope we'll never get to that pitch of things!' I certainly hope *I* never will. We are talking about what happens in 'survival' conditions, after all, and we all aim to avoid those like the plague—but it is as well to have a few built-in saving factors to one's boat, all the same. It is very nice to know, however, that in actual practice this business of being 'thrown over on beam ends' seems to happen to catamarans very rarely indeed.

Even in ocean storms, catamarans fitted with these long, shallow keels ride away from the big bursting crests without heeling unduly, because the keels are still, relatively speaking, in the surface water which is highly aerated in such conditions. Both the Prout designed Ocean Ranger and the smaller Snowgoose 34 (not to mention several Ranger 27s and 31s) have proved this in deep-water gales, so, if a catamaran needs to have external keels of one sort or another it would look as if deep fins are not ideal; centreboards are better (and will give probably the best windward performance in a strong wind provided you will take the risk of keeping them down); and all round long shallow keels may be the answer. But not all hull forms require such 'outside assistance' in order to have a satisfactory windward performance for cruising; a well designed 'V' underwater section, as in Wharram's boats and the Catalac and others can make sufficient of a 'leeway barrier' of themselves, yet will side-slip safely if ever they were to be heeled (and I can find no records of such a thing happening to any of them, curiously enough, though I don't *think* that proves anything).

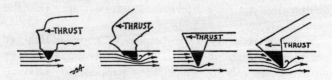

WATER FLOW UNDER 'V'HULLS AT EXTREME ANGLES OF HEEL

WATER BALLAST

To get back to self-righting keels. Ballasted ones. Bill O'Brien dreamed up an answer to some of the problems of ballast without weight—which is the ideal for a cat. His Channel Rover was originally fitted with a pivoted centreboard of fat, streamlined section, which was hollow. Small holes allowed the keel to fill slowly when it was lowered into the water in the normal way. Then, if the boat was heeled sufficiently, the keel would gradually come out of the water, carrying its load of water into the air, so as to right the boat before it had time to drain.

There were drawbacks, though. For one thing, anything (keel, dagger-board, outboard engine) sticking into the water centrally between the hulls of a catamaran collects all the seaweed and flotsam that is going. All this muck gets diverted down the middle because the two inward flowing bow-waves tend to throw everything just there, and I would imagine that this might be a serious drawback with this type of keel. On top of that, a necessarily wide keel like this is bound to have its own wave-making properties at the surface, which must be detrimental to performance. There is no doubt that even with relatively thin wooden dagger-boards fitted centrally between the hulls, the early Shearwater III racing cats were not as fast as those with the same rig but later fitted with twin boards, one through each hull.

A further snag was the amount of space which the casing which housed O'Brien's 'water-keel' in its raised position took up on the bridgedeck. In Channel Rover it was so cumbersome in saloon and cockpit (even though some of it was down in a 'pod' or nacelle) that it was eventually scrapped as an idea, keel-less boats from the same moulds being rerigged as ketches instead of sloops and called the Amazon class.

DODGES AND DEVICES

All sorts of other anticapsize devices have been mooted, and even tried. Some very surprising indeed. One European designer has experimented with, of all things, elastic chain-plates (for want of an easier way to explain them). The idea is that under pressure from the wind, the rig will gradually heel over as it would in a monohull, leaving the boat upright beneath it. It will thus spill wind and relieve pressure 'naturally' without the sheets having to be eased in a squall. I can only think that the resulting increase of weight over the lee side of the boat as the mast and so on lean that way can hardly be an ideal to strive for, but maybe I have misunderstood something.

People have suggested other things, ranging from inflatable bags arranged along each side-deck, to help roll a knocked-down cat back upright, to solid floats placed on extra wide crosstrees about half way up the mast. These would certainly have an advantage over 'conventional' masthead floats in that the latter let the boat lie at an angle beyond 90 degrees off the vertical so that her

Centre of Gravity comes the wrong side of her Centre of Buoyancy, requiring the end of the mast to be lifted some three to five feet before the boat will right herself. Floats on wide enough crosstree ends would overcome this one, but the windage in normal sailing must be awful, and the rigging involved in ensuring that the things didn't rip off at the roots when the boat capsized at speed would hardly help. (Extra rigging would not be needed if inflatable floats were used instead of permanent ones up there.)

6

Seamanship Safety

Except for the press-on-or-bust racing maniac, or perhaps the chap with a cranky boat, there is no reason why a catamaran should ever find herself upside down. Common sense and prudent seamanship are the proper defence, and there is really no need for elaborate safety gadgets. Just the ordinary safety gear carried by any well found yacht is all a cat needs, though naturally seamanship may be aided by the right choice of fittings.

JAM-CLEATS

The first of these is to have really good jam-cleats on all sheets. On my own catamaran I use two types: the crab-like 'Cam Cleat' and the modern, grooved-and-ridged 'v' fittings called 'Clam Cleats'. With either type, a smart tug on the sheet releases it instantly. '(The ordinary cleat with a nipping wedge under one arm is not ideal, because even one round turn takes longer to undo than a straight pull.)

On those rare occasions when in sudden squalls we may find ourselves carrying sufficient canvas to make the weather hull 'go light', the helmsman, if alone on deck, brings the ends of the working sheets to where he is sitting, so that he has instant control if things become exciting. But I should point out how rarely this is necessary. In many thousands of miles of catamaran cruising, sometimes in viciously gusty conditions, I have deemed it wise to release a sheet maybe four or five times, and (so far as I am aware) have never lifted a weather hull *completely* clear of the wave-tops. I'll say it again:

Capsizing is not one of the risks one need ever run when sailing in cruising catamarans.

PREVENTION—BETTER THAN CURE

Obviously it is better to prevent the onset of trouble, than to rely on curing it once it has already happened. The best—and easiest—method of preventing a knock-down is to apply sensible seamanship from the outset; and that does not mean being perpetually undercanvassed. (Even the *Haxted Argo II* capsize could *theoretically* have been avoided, had she hove-to outside the Elbe until the ebb had *completely* finished running—though it is quite understandable why this was not done at the time!)

Apart from detailed navigation and course-planning and timing, in order to avoid exceptional or freak sea conditions as far as possible, the remaining risk of knock-down comes from being caught momentarily overcanvassed in a gust or squall—which can happen to us all. And then the quick release of sheets, coupled with an ability to reduce sail rapidly and efficiently, is the only sensible answer.

YOU KNOW WHEN YOU'RE PUSHING HER

Easily released sheets are one thing, and the simplest method of all; but there are other refinements which can help the cruising man. It can sometimes be thought diffi-

Above : The 26-foot Heavenly Twins centre-cockpit catamaran. Steered from just abaft the mast, she represents what a true cruising boat should be: easy to handle, compact and comfortable.
(Photo: Colin Rowe)

Below : One of the smallest of the range: the 22-foot Hirondelle, seen here making off down the Solent at her usual astonishing speed.
(Photo: Jim Andrews)

Above: The 27-foot Ranger *Twintail,* which carried the Andrews family happily over some 4,000 miles of coastal waters, seen here in the tranquility of Strangford Lough.

Below: *Twintail* on a beam reach in the Firth of Clyde, sledging smoothly along bolt upright at nine knots, while a friend relaxes at the helm. (*Photos: Jim Andrews*)

Above: The 9-metre Catalac which replaced *Twintail* as our family grew. Calm reflections show her transoms clear of the water, and shadows display her chine bows and flaring topsides. Note too the recessed steering position.

Below: On board *Aku-Aku* at seven knots, close-hauled in Force 5-6 in the English Channel. The helmsman sits dry and snug under the hood, and the large sliding hatch lets light and air into the saloon.
(Photos: Jim Andrews)

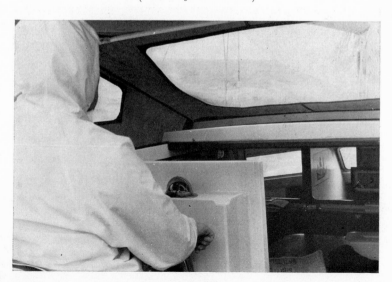

Above: The huge saloon in the Prouts' Snowgoose 34, showing the foot-well and extra headroom provided by her central 'nacelle'. To starboard, forward of the magnificent galley, is the door to a double-berth forecabin. (*Photo: Jim Andrews*)

Below: A gathering of Bobcats in St. Helier, Jersey. These comfortable and very safe cruising boats have given endless fun to literally hundreds of families. (*Photo: Tom Lack*)

cult for people who are either new to catamarans or to sailing in general, to know just *when* a catamaran is becoming over-pressed. She may be going jolly fast on, say, a close-reach, and yet heeling less than eight degrees or so. How then does one tell if one is pushing her too hard?

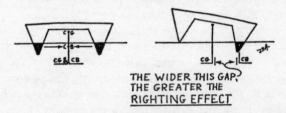

THE WIDER THIS GAP,
THE GREATER THE
RIGHTING EFFECT

Experience of that particular boat will teach you, of course—but that is no use during your first season or two. However, one can always *feel* the boat began to strain and, as it were, 'go tense' when she's nearing the time for a sail-change. But more clearly, when a hull starts to rise from the water, the angle of heel itself will prove you are grossly overdoing things, though even at that stage there is no need for fear—the boat is still immensely stable. The trouble is that once a catamaran's weather hull is properly 'unstuck', there *may* only be a few seconds in which to save the situation, and the angle, from becoming acute.

SHEET-RELEASE GEAR

Either you arrange, in such conditions, that there is some-one who can *instantly* release the sheets without fail if the need should arise, or you fit some really reliable automatic sheet-release gear. Such things are available on the market, and the more costly ones are excellent.

It is all a matter of how much one is prepared to spend for this kind of peace of mind—*if* you are habitually either going to sail the boat so near her limits, or if you are going to leave the deck in charge of inexperienced or irresponsible people (and by 'irresponsible' in this instance, I mean those who may not be capable of recognising the danger of a situation in time to act early enough with their own hands).

It is not everyone who races their cruising boat regularly, but most families thoroughly enjoy the odd bash round the buoys once or twice a year. There is certainly no better way to learn how to get the best out of one's sails. For that sort of short, occasional event, where everyone is on hand with the sheets anyway, I see no need for expensive gadgetry—nor even for specially large winches to cope with the pull of vast racing headsails.

More serious racing is of course a very different matter. Such equipment is then needed in order to do well—and I believe that really good automatic sheet-release gear, masthead floats and anything else, should be fitted to lessen the nagging worry which would otherwise assail a skipper who knew he was driving his cat right at her limits and maybe leaving nothing at all in hand for that extra puff ...

But the family man is often short-handed, and it therefore behoves him to have something other than just his jam-cleats to rely on. (Particularly if he has any doubts about recognising when his ship is becoming overpressed.)

SHORTEN SAIL EARLY

One answer is to choose jibsheet winches which are not quite powerful enough to bring in a big headsail when the wind is really fresh. It so happens that boats like most of the smaller production catamarans are mostly supplied as standard with 'minimum power' sheet winches. (Bigger ones are expensive.)

I used to think this was nothing but a nuisance, and wished for tougher, more powerful winches so that my wife and daughters could handle the sheets easily even in a breeze. To a point, of course, they *should* be able to do so, and perhaps on *Twintail* anyway we could well have had the next size of winch up, and still been able to carry the relatively far more efficient area in our head-sails in fresher winds without over-pressing her.

In our present boat, a Catalac, the standard winches are just about right as safety features, in that by the time a given headsail is nearing the point of overloading the ship, it is also becoming very difficult to winch in when tacking, and it is therefore *necessary* to change to something smaller. The sizes of the respective headsails has something to do with it, of course. In the Catalac it so happens that, with full mainsail, the 232 sq. ft. genoa becomes difficult to sheet at just the right moment when one should anyway change to the working jib of 145 sq. ft. And that in turn becomes too hard to sheet home only after two deep reefs have been tied in the main.

How do we know when to reef the main? Weather helm is the indicator there—she becomes harder to hold. The same sort of thing applies to most production cata-marans, but really, it's a bit like the question of how fast one should drive a car round a given corner—you just *know*.

I do not believe that deliberate undercanvassing at the design stage is necessarily the right approach, because in doing that you virtually destroy the boat's perform-ance in light going—the very condition in which most of us do our sailing from choice. It is surely on those quiet days, especially at the ends of the season, when the most pleasant sailing of all can be had; nosing into creeks and anchorages, pottering about for the sheer fun of it. It therefore seems to me almost criminal to cripple a boat under those idyllic conditions by giving her such short spars that it is impossible for her to carry adequate sail. Not that I am advocating *long* masts, because a tall rig on a catamaran is *not* an advantage.

BIG, LIGHT-WEATHER SAILS

A yacht should be able to crowd on plenty of sail in light airs, so that her crew does not for ever have to resort to the racket of an engine every time the breeze falls below Force 2. The point is that if her winches are bordering on the inadequate, rather than the all-efficient, powerful kind of machinery needed in racing craft, the cruising cat can safely carry vast headsails because as soon as they put enough strain on the winches to make sheeting difficult, one *has* to change down to something smaller, and it will be about time to do that anyway.

FRANGIBLE SHEET COUPLINGS

One could, however, have a steadily increasing wind without the need to touch the winches and not know they were becoming overloaded. To overcome this with large fore-and-aft headsails (not spinnakers), the sheets can be attached to the sail with a length of light twine, a given number of turns only being taken to secure them (worked out by trial and error). Then, if the relative wind-speed reaches, say, twelve knots, the twine parts and 'automatically' releases the sheet. When the panic is over, it doesn't take a minute on the broad foredeck of a cata-maran to make all fast with a new length of twine—same number of turns, of course.

KNIVES, AND THE NEED FOR THEM

Should it ever actually be necessary to release sheets sud-denly, since a headsail is roughly twice as efficient and powerful as a sail set abaft the mast, *when the wind is forward of the beam* the headsail is the one to let fly first. (Unless a very small headsail is being carried with the full mainsail.) However, nowadays almost all headsails are sheeted round winches, and on even the best positioned of these a sheet can jam (as indeed happened in *Golden Cockerel*). For that reason every catamaran skipper should carry a razor-sharp sheath-knife at his belt, or else have one positioned permanently in the cockpit, where it can be whipped out instantly to slice through a jammed sheet.

But I say again; with a bit of normal care and common sense, anything even approaching a capsize should never begin to happen. Ah—but *supposing* it does—what then?

AFTER THE BALL IS OVER...

First of all, let's assume that our poor cat is fitted with some kind of masthead buoyancy, and it did work and didn't fall off in the hour of need. The boat will then be lying on her side, mast angled just beyond the hori-zontal, so that the weather hull (that was) has come up over, *beyond* the balance-point of the lower one on which she rests. She will now seem unlikely to right herself unaided. However, if it has happened in something of a sea, then there is in fact more than a little chance that in a moment or two the hull might drop into a trough while the masthead is lifted on a crest, and she is then quite likely to come up, particularly if her safety-harnessed crew can assist in any way.

LET IN SOME WATER?

In the case of *Haxted Argo II* a lot of water got inside, so that the lee hull was allowed to sink lower in the water, thus bringing the mast nearer the horizontal. Failing other means of righting her, this might be something to do *purposely*, but only if the boat has been fitted with adequate foam or other buoyancy. She naturally must be quite unsinkable when flooded, or the job will have to be done with very great care. Water could be bailed in—and bailed out again when she was up on her feet once more.

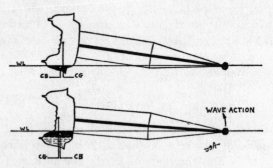

DELIBERATE HULL-FLOODING CAN BRING THE CENTRE OF GRAVITY BACK THE RIGHT SIDE OF THE CENTRE OF BUOYANCY

STAY WITH HER

In the last resort, there is always this: even if she resists all attempts to be righted, she cannot sink if fitted with enough buoyancy. And even if not fitted with *any* buoyancy other than at the masthead, so long as excessive water can be prevented from entering, she should remain afloat indefinitely—a large and highly visible and decidedly unusual looking object, alone upon the sea. So one should *stay with her*. If at all possible, stay on or even in her, until help comes. She will be a lot easier to find than a tiny life-raft or rubber dinghy. (As a further precaution, more than one ocean-going catamaran has had the underside of her bridgedeck pessimistically painted Air/Sea Rescue Orange.)

TOTAL FLIP, AND WHAT TO DO ABOUT IT

Much the same things apply if she does the Very Awful, and inverts completely ... Even the cat not fitted with *any* kind of buoyancy will remain afloat upside-down, so long as air trapped inside is not allowed to escape through seacocks or other apertures. I gather that this was the case with *Golden Cockerel*, and it was reported that some of her crew members were for a while clambering about inside the inverted craft shutting off all skin-fittings as far as possible, before swimming out to join their pals on the big steady raft which had once been the bottom of the bridgedeck.

To those who had been below, the experience had apparently been one excruciating moment when they knew she was going over, then all the roaring stopped, and 'everything went quiet' and relatively peaceful, which gave them time to think about what to do. There seemed to them no desperate rush to go out topsides into the cold and wet, though naturally those who had been out there, and had worked out clear of sheets and life-lines (and safety harnesses, which I'll come to in a moment), must have been very worried until everyone turned up safely. For them there was no question of having to wait long to be rescued, since they were right under the land, and dozens of people saw it all happen. But even had they been at sea, the impression is that they would have had ample opportunity to do things about survival until somebody did show up who could perhaps help them.

DOUBLE-CLIP HARNESSES

A most unpleasant thought is that of struggling away underwater below a capsized cockpit or foredeck, trying to release the far end of a safety harness. This has happened—and the suggestion is that catamariners should perhaps use safety harnesses which have clips at both ends of the harness rope. That way you could always unclip yourself, which would be quicker than hacking through the line with that sheath-knife, as anyone who has tried working underwater will know.

LIFE-RAFT ACCESSIBILITY

While on this dreadful but most *unlikely* subject of being inverted, one other thing is perhaps worth thinking about. If a life-raft is carried, it should be so positioned as to be easily accessible, whether the boat is upside-down or rightway-up; slung between the sterns, for instance, or on the foredeck trampoline or netting if she is the sort of cat which needs space-fillers of that kind between the hulls. By the same token, a portable emergency transmitter might be similarly sited when at sea.

CREW ERROR—THE MAIN RISK

It is true to say, however, that all the capsizes of which

I have found record, have happened either whilst racing, or as a result of poor seamanship or wrong calculations (however understandable) in exceptionally severe conditions, either on the part of the navigator, the crew on watch, or (rarely) on the part of the designers and builders when the crew were not capable of seeing the arising danger. In very few instances could any one of these factors be entirely blamed by itself, but there can be no doubt at all that a certain very ancient Seafaring Saying can most appropriately be applied. 'It ain't the ships; it's the men in 'em.'

Catamarans—even quite little ones—have ridden out most vicious storms at sea. There are many techniques to be employed then, and some are suggested in the chapter on Handling.

Two further things noticeably affect the capsizability of a catamaran. These are the Windage of hull and rig, and Weight Distribution. Let's look at windage first.

HULL WINDAGE

All hulls (and rigs) have drag characteristics, and to some extent I have touched upon the underwater drag and the effect which that can have in causing or preventing capsize. The above-water design of a catamaran can be allowed to differ considerably from that of a conventional heeling monohull, simply because a non-heeling catamaran does not, for instance, need the sort of topsides which a heeling boat *must* have if helm balance is to be retained when she rolls over and deeply immerses one side for long periods. In other words, the topside shape of a catamaran is going to be influenced by the same (or nearly the same) things that influence the design of a pure motor-cruiser. So there are few reasons why the above-water profile of a catamaran should not *look* very like that of a motor-yacht.

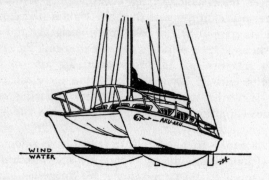

HULL WINDAGE & GRIP

An important difference, of course, is that whereas the motor yacht will be driven to windward by the burning of liquid fuel and appropriate machinery, the sailing catamaran will be driven to windward by the wind—so there is a rather greater need for the general windage, or 'air-drag' to be kept as low as possible. At the same time, adequate freeboard forward is very important in this type of craft; the two require careful compromising.

BRIDGDECK WINDAGE (We have Lift-Off ...!)

In highly extreme winds, the design of the connecting bridgedeck structure may have great bearing on the craft's stability, in that if the wing-deck is so designed that it can produce aerodynamic lift—an exceptional squall even when the craft is at anchor (never mind caught in the act of leaping off the top of a crest at sea), might supposedly be enough to cause her to take off and then be blown over. Obviously, the more super-structural windage (cabin-top, masts, rigging, and so on) there is, the more some part of the hull is likely to lift and let the wind get in under her. Then there is something to be said for the slatted or at least short bridge-deck with netting or webbing 'trampolines' between the bows or sterns.

My own feeling about this is that as far as windage and lift are concerned, the sort of solid bridgedeck which continues right up or nearly up to the ends of the boat is *not* dangerous in this way, so long as it is given a proper aerofoil fore-and-aft section designed like an *upside-down* aircraft wing, the effect of which in such savage, once-in-a-lifetime squalls, would if anything be to help hold the boat *down*. But I could be wrong.

I have never noticed any tendency of either of my relatively long bridgedecked catamarans to become air-borne, even when anchored in winds measured well in excess of eighty knots, though mast windage has occasionally caused a 'rearing' sensation.

WINDAGE ON TOPHAMPER

Windage on the superstructure and rig of course has its tipping moment—something more against having fixed masthead buoyancy, I suppose. And if you think that a few extra wires or strings up and down the mast to support it or hoist sails etc., won't make much difference, some day when there's a good breeze blowing, take hold of the extreme end of a long bamboo stick, or something of the kind, and hold it up vertically as high as you can in the wind. The windage is surprising.

This suggests that catamaran rigging should be kept as

simple as possible, provided it is still able to cope with
the fierce loading and deflections caused by the non-heeling hull. It is, no doubt, a strong case for internal halyards, though personally I can't abide the things (and
don't have them on my own boat).

WEIGHT DISTRIBUTION

When it comes to weight distribution, I think it best
to quote from Nigel Tetley's *'Trimaran Solo'* (Nautical
Publishing Company, 1970): 'Next to sheer speed, in
Victress's case, I reckon weight distribution the most
important aspect in limiting the risk of capsize.'

Wise words, even with mere catamarans in mind!

KEEP WEIGHT OFF THE BOW

One has to bear in mind where the forces of the rig are
heading; somewhere over the lee bow, or forwards, at
any rate. I have often noticed that when motoring in a
flat calm, both *Twintail*, and to a lesser extent, *Aku-Aku*,
used to increase speed by maybe a quarter of a knot or so
if someone went right forward and stood on either bow.
I have also noticed that when one does this with the boat
under sail, the effect is either absent or even opposite.
Try going forward in one of the delightful little Hirondelle catamarans when she is under sail, and she will
instantly lose as much as a knot. Under power this is not
the case.

Under engine, most boats of whatever shape tend to
squat down aft—so therefore the weight of the crew going
forward merely restores her to her proper trim—her designed waterline. But under sail what happens? The sails
tend to push her masthead forwards, the backstays hold

on to and try to lift the stern, and her head is pushed down. The greater the wind thrust, the deeper go her bows. Almost any lee-side photograph of any catamaran going well under sail even with the wind *forward* of the beam, will show the bow to be more deeply immersed than the stern. Send crew weight forward, or place any weight up there, and obviously one has at once made the matter worse. As mentioned earlier on, this will almost certainly make the boat heavy on the helm and tend to gripe round to weather all the time, which in turn makes one throw the rudders into permanent action, slowing her up.

Not that I am suggesting that *all* weight should be stowed aft of amidships in a cat. They are usually designed to carry *some* additional gear forward. And there is no point in stacking everything aft, since that would likely give her *lee* helm instead! Which also has its dangers.

In loading stores and water on board any catamaran, and particularly the smaller ones, where the amount of added weight is usually a larger proportion of the final all-up weight of the boat, the important thing to remember is to keep the waterline trim level, or if anything *slightly* down by the stern—NEVER down by the bow. From this point of view, the 26-foot Heavenly Twins centre-cockpit design by Pat Patterson has great advantages.

KEEP THE HEAVIES LOW

By the same token of common-sense, obviously the lower any weight can be kept, the more stable the boat will be in a blow or steep, beam-on sea. I would hesitate to stow even a small quantity of water on the bridgedeck if I

could by any means avoid doing so. The same applies
to fuel, anchor chains, spare anchors, and so forth. However, if for any reason things like that do have to be
stowed on the bridgedeck or cabin-top or at deck level
—high above the waterline, in other words—then the
only thing one can do to lessen the dangers imposed is to
keep those weights as near the centreline as possible;
never out to the side. Auxiliary engines are often a case
in point.

CREW WEIGHT (*Impersonal!*)

As to the crew themselves, well, clearly in a large cat it
isn't going to make much difference having even a fairly
heavy chap trotting around the ship. In a little catamaran though, it *is* going to matter—and more than one
might think.

For this reason, I much prefer in a small catamaran
to have a washroom and toilet compartment positioned
aft of amidships, and not—definitely not—up in one
bow. The weight of the average adult is a noticeable proportion of the weight of a small unballasted catamaran,
and a short-waterline catamaran is going to dip quite
readily whatever end that adult goes to.

In tougher moments anyhow, maybe during a sudden
squall or when 'pushing' the boat hard for any reason,
the prudent skipper will tell his crew to keep clear of
the lee bow, and in *very* small catamarans will try to keep
them aft and to weather, until things have eased, or
sail can be reduced.

BALANCE THE TRIM ALL ROUND

Where 'thwartships trim is concerned, clearly if one hull

is more heavily laden than the other, the boat will be a lot stiffer and more stable when that happens to be the windward wide. (Racing catamariners have been known to shift water cans over into the windward hull to take advantage of this.)

When there is more weight in the lee hull than in the weather one, provided it is low down below the water-line it won't make much difference, except that any tendency of the lee hull to 'knife-in' will be increased. Naturally, the boat would be more stable if some weight were then distributed into the weather hull as well. In other words, one should try to stow her so that the weight is as equal as can be in both hulls, keep it as low as possible, and avoid utterly even the slightest bow-down trimming in a sailing catamaran.

As with any other type of sailing, common sense is always the key safety factor. Forget to apply that at any moment, and you have at once a potentially dangerous ship. Remember to apply common sense in a catamaran, and you quite possibly have one of the safest boats man has ever devised.

THE LONE HAND

What of the single-hander? There have to be times when he is not at the helm—when he is sleeping, maybe. He can fit automatic sheet-release gear if he has the money, or he can see that he never carries too much sail. Like *any* catamaran sailor, he should always reef early and sail with something in hand for the puffs. To quote Nigel Tetley once again:

'It is doubtful whether a single-hander will ever be able to exploit a multihull's full speed potential in the Roaring Forties—in safety anyhow.'

I agree with him, though I don't think the Roaring Forties need have been singled out for that comment— he just happened to have been there at the time he made it!

7

Hull Shapes and
Constructions

I have already said a good deal about hull shapes in relation to safety, for it is the shape and construction of any
type of boat which renders it seaworthy or otherwise.
But the wide variations of build and form give the pros-
pective catamaran owner a considerable choice of
features, ranging from the sturdily robust, to shapes ideal
for specialised high-speed sailing. The construction provides the strength and flexibility, or the solidity; the
shape determines the overall performance.

PERFORMANCE CHARACTERISTICS

In a recent cruiser race, I was able with great interest
to observe, under very strong winds, the behaviour of two
similarly sized catamarans. Conditions were Force 6 gusting well into Force 7 in the sheltered waters of the Firth
of Clyde. So there were virtually no big seas. The two
boats were my own Catalac, and an Aristocat. Both
designs to some extent were conceived from the same
basic ideas, the Aristocat being intended as a high-performance cruiser-racer, while the Catalac is an out-and-
out cruiser. The general dimensions and the accommodation plans are nevertheless roughly similar, as indeed

are the rigs, but there any likenesses end, for the actual designs are miles apart.

The Catalac is very much aimed at pure cruising comfort and the ability to get you where you want with the maximum ease and shelter and minimum of fuss. The Aristocat design also offers luxurious accommodation, but less shelter for the on-watch crew and helmsman, and a bit more work to do besides. The Catalac has powerful chines and the hulls are basically 'V'-sectioned; the Aristocat is 'U'-sectioned. The Catalac has no form of keel appendages, her hull shape being enough to reduce leeway in normal conditions to an acceptable degree; the Aristocat, because of her 'U' hulls, has to have something and was designed with a large drop-keel in each hull.

Off the wind, although at that time the Aristocat was carrying full mainsail and working jib, whereas our working jib was carried along with a single deeply reefed mainsail, the Aristocat dropped steadily further and further astern. There was no doubt that with our shorter waterline length and smaller sail area, only the underwater shape of the Catalac could be giving us this advantage.

However, as soon as we rounded the leeward mark and came hard on the wind, the Aristocat came sweeping up on us again, not only pointing higher in those conditions, but travelling a fraction faster into the bargain, for all that our Sumlog showed a persistent six to seven knots, and more in the gusts. In every squall, our leeway (unhindered by any form of keel or centreboard) increased visibly, and we rode the gusts easily. But our windward performance in such harsh conditions was obviously not a match for that of the other boat (even when we tucked in another reef without loss of speed), despite the fact that we had trounced her well and truly on the downwind leg.

And here, perhaps, is the difference between a boat designed purely for cruising, and one designed at least partly with racing in mind. I could not help feeling that the strains on our hull and rigging in those vicious gusts were considerably lessened by the boat's lack of resistance to leeway when sailing in highly disturbed, aerated water. And since that day, I have discovered that some Aristocats have suffered damage to their drop-keel cases as a direct result of the forces imposed on a non-heeling hull with high, leeway-resistance appendages. In the squalls, the Aristocat we were racing hardly heeled any further than our own eight degrees, but she made no noticeable increase in leeway, so the stresses on hulls, rudders, drop-keels and especially the rig and rigging must indeed have been greater. Not that anything broke, so far as we were aware!

Certainly she got home before us, for there were only the two legs to that particular race, and the windward one was four times the length of the run. There was no question of the Catalac failing to go to windward, or anything like that. We made what I considered to be a completely satisfying and very rapid progress towards the finish, despite having nothing other than the deep 'V' shape of our hulls to stop us sliding sideways. It is interesting all the same to note that in more normal conditions, of say around Force 5 and under, the Catalac points high and makes usually around five degrees of leeway.

THE PERFORMANCE YOU WANT...

To me, the fact that I want a pure cruising boat is the important thing. And when you cruise with the idea of using a free wind and not beating more than you have to (who *does* want to beat, when cruising?), a boat with a high performance downwind is obviously going to be more satisfactory than one which is slower except when beating. If you race, it's different. So long as the windward performance is adequate to get me upwind at a reasonable pace, surely and steadily, and sufficient to take me out of trouble, I personally am satisfied.

Other folk worry more about how their boat will perform against the glossy ocean racers, for that is how they get their fun, and maybe the business of working gently into some narrow creek under sail, or drifting through 'rafts' of guillemots and razorbills on the calm peace of the Sea of the Hebrides is to them a tame and boring idea.

The thing is to know what hull and rig features are going to give which type of performance, and how to judge that is what this book sets out to try and show. The Aristocat/Catalac example happens to be a handy one for me to recount. There are, of course, many other hull forms and so on, which could be compared similarly to demonstrate other points. I am by no means saying that if you want a racing/cruiser, choose an Aristocat, or that there is no better true cruiser than a Catalac. I am merely attempting to say in just one more way, that it is well worth considering just what type of sailing you personally wish mostly to indulge in, before choosing your boat.

'V' HULLS

The cheapest form of wood construction lies undoubtedly in making use of plywood panels. This, almost willy-nilly, means 'V'-bottomed hulls. Box-sectioned, flat bottomed hulls have never proved successful in catamarans, owing to their high-drag characteristics. There are, however, several good forms of 'V' hulls, and one or two not-so-good ones. The worst from the safety angle (though it is excellent from a performance point of view) is a very steep sided, narrow 'V', which may be either symmetrical or asymmetrical with one side of the 'V' vertical and the other leaning inwards towards the craft's centreline. With the outboard side of each hull vertical, one has the maximum possible straddle-stability and resistance to leeway.

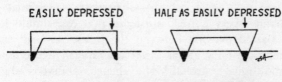

EASILY DEPRESSED   HALF AS EASILY DEPRESSED

LOAD-BEARING CHARACTERISTICS

The snag is that this kind of narrow section has horribly little reserve buoyancy, and can therefore easily be depressed—which rather counteracts the extra width of the 'straddle'. Moreover, as stated earlier, this shape, particularly if asymmetrically arranged, will not skid sideways when heeled excessively in the way that other hull forms can, and so may capsize more readily. *Golden Cockerel* and *Imi Loa*, two American designs of this type, have gone over in this way (both when racing).

The next kind of 'V' hull is perhaps the simplest of all, and is a shape developed and greatly favoured by British designer James Wharram. It is a straightforward, un-adulterated 'V' section, of such an angle at the keel as to provide fairly adequate resistance to leeway while upright, yet which will slip sideways to ride the punch of ocean storm-waves, amidst which the idea was originally conceived.

This skin of plywood, suitably reinforced with stringers and bulkheads within the hulls and rising from well rockered keelsons, is immensely strong, and so easy to put together that the vast majority of Wharram catamarans are home-built in back-yards, fields, and fore-shores all over the world.

Again there are drawbacks. The main one here is that such a narrow hull at the level of the cabin-sole affords very restricted living accommodation and but little stow-age space—a fact which is further aggravated by Wharram's very correct insistence that one should have only slatted decking between the hulls (no bridgedeck accommodation at all) and that any superstructure should be absolutely minimal. The theory is that a slatted bridgedeck will not generate lift in storm-winds, and seas can burst harmlessly between the hulls without any pounding taking place. Wharram places great impor-tance on this for his ocean-going craft (which most of them are), and to bear it out, I believe it is true to say that the only cruising catamarans of his design which have ever been capsized have had modifications done to incorporate bridgedeck accommodation—which seems to prove something.

RIGID OR FLEXIBLE?

This, before going on to the third type of 'V' hull, seems to be the best moment to discuss the business of flexible *versus* solid monocoque construction, since it is Jim Wharram who favours the former.

It works like this. Whereas most 'production' catamarans are built in such a way that their hulls, bridge-decks, decking, cockpits and cabin-tops are all connected up and stiffened with beams and box-girders and ath-wartships bulkheads so as to move as one solid unit, flex-ible construction is so designed as to let the two hulls of the boat 'waggle' (a bit) in an up-and-down sense. To put it another way; while the two hulls of a flexible catamaran are prevented by tie-beams from diverging in any way, there is enough movement permitted by the beams of a flexible boat and their special fixing points, to enable the bow of one hull to ride up on a wave while the other bow stays down.

The idea is two-fold. By so flexing in a seaway, there is seemingly less drag than with a boat which has to to move all of a piece, no matter what the seas are trying to make each bit of her do. Secondly, and far more importantly, when the wind in the rig sends its thrust out and down over the lee bow, the lee bow of a flexibly connected pair of hulls need not depress deeply, as would that of a more solidly constructed vessel. Instead it is capable of 'riding up' in relation to the rest of the craft, putting her, if you like, into a kind of diagonal twist. This does not seem to affect her speed in any adverse way, partly because with no bow digging in to destroy the hull balance by shifting the CLR drastically forward as in a monocoque cat, the flexible boat's helm remains light. The fact that the movement is very slight, and yet achieves a difference, is of interest. That, anyway, is the theory behind it, if I understand it correctly.

RIG PROBLEMS

The same idea has been tried out by Rodney Macalpine-Downie, who is known for such very high performance cats as the Iroquois and Apache. His experimental Mirrorcat design consists of two very enlarged Iroquois-type hulls (each with its own little cabintop), held apart by tubular beams and a box-girder under the central mast-step. Being exceptionally light, this boat is capable of very high speeds indeed, but the problems of keeping the rigging taut and in sensible tension-balance without jerking the mast when the hulls move in relation to one-another are very great, and in heavy seas I understand these difficulties become fairly serious.

All catamarans suffer from certain rigging problems, because of the tremendous compression strains which their non-heeling hulls inevitably impose in hard going. It becomes almost impossible, for instance, to keep mast-head forestays and the luff of a big jib tight and straight. Even metal masts seem to shorten noticeably under the strain—though in reality the distortion is in the bridge-deck or cabintop on which the mast is stepped. For that reason catamaran headsails should be cut flatter than those of monohulls. But when the hulls are moving 'separately', the problem is even greater.

In the Wharram catamaran's case, however, the rigs themselves are usually designed to be flexible, since Jim Wharram is concerned with cruising safety rather than with racing efficiency, so it doesn't matter so much if the whole thing wallops about somewhat, so long as it holds together. With most Wharram designs, therefore, the problem of how to keep a tight luff on the genoa just doesn't arise.

His idea is that rather than put terrific compression strains on spars and high tension on rigging, the rig should itself, rather like a tree in a gale, bend before the wind. This of course, coupled with his mistrust of centreboards or other keels where catamarans are concerned, may make his craft a bit uncertain to windward in very extreme conditions. But Jim Wharram is first of all a seaman, and he maintains that with a reasonable amount of prudence, one need not often get one's boat into such a position as to necessitate beating in gale-force winds.

Jim Wharram has many ideas which for a long, long time have been treated with some scorn by other multi-hull designers, though now more and more of them are beginning to explore some of the same ground which he has already covered. One of the American CSK designs which has recently been proving far more successful than their previous asymmetrical hulls, has been a narrow, symmetrical 'V' shape not at all unlike some of the more sporty Wharram versions. Curiously enough, this boat was named *Polynesian Concept* (*Polycon*, for short). Wharram has always described his designs as being of 'Polynesian' origin. (See Chapter 12 on Historical Origins.)

THE SAME AT BOTH ENDS

The basic Wharram catamaran, then, is made up of twin 'V'-shaped hulls, held apart by flexibly mounted beams, the spaces between them being decked with separated slats of timber so as to offer the crests of ocean storm seas least resistance. The hull profile, as seen from the side, is also very simple, a heavily rockered keel rising to the forefoot where a straight, well-raked stempost is matched at the other end by an almost similarly raked sternpost, on which the rudder is hung (one to each hull, as in most cats).

The sterns are pointed, just like the bows, Jim Wharram's theory being that when a wave lifts one end, the

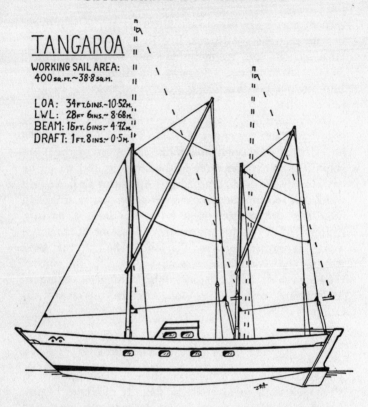

TANGAROA

WORKING SAIL AREA:
400 sq.ft. ~ 38.8 sq.m.

LOA: 34 ft. 6 ins. ~ 10.52 m.
LWL: 28 ft. 6 ins. ~ 8.68 m.
BEAM: 16 ft. 6 ins. ~ 4.72 m.
DRAFT: 1 ft. 8 ins. ~ 0.5 m.

forces of buoyancy are matched more or less exactly at the other end, so that the hulls remain in end-for-end balance all the time. This would naturally cut down drag, and (in theory) should prevent excessive pitching. In practice, however, it has been discovered that the pitching qualities can be radically altered with different rigs, so this aspect needs a good deal more understanding yet.

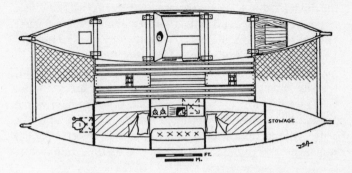

TANGAROA. Designed by J. Wharram; sold by Polynesian Catamarans, The Longhouse, Milford Docks, Milford Haven, Pembrokeshire, South Wales. (Plans and materials also from Bromley Boats, 109/123 Southlands Road, Bromley, Kent, England.) Plywood sheet construction, designed for easy D.I.Y. No keels, relies on hull shape and small skegs aft to reduce leeway. Fixed-draft rudders. Tiller steering. Outboard motor. Somewhat spartan accommodation, sleeping 2 adults in each hull. Open, slatted bridgedeck. Hulls flexibly connected.

More a passage-maker than a creek-crawler. Extremely seaworthy and stable. Simple rig. Others in range include 22-foot Hine and Hine Moa, 27.5-foot Tane, 40-foot Narai, 45-foot Oro, and 51-foot Tehini.

Generally speaking, the Wharram type of hull is perhaps more ideal for ocean wandering than for coastal pottering when manoeuvrability is more the thing, and there can be no doubt whatever that hundreds—maybe thousands—of people have had a very great deal of pleasure out of their Wharram 'Polynesian' catamarans in all sorts of conditions imaginable, and invariably write enthusiastically to tell him how well they have found the boats behave when the weather turns wicked. The sense of security and safety at sea which these rather specialised designs afford is obviously very marked indeed. It is also worth noting that by doing the work yourself, you can have a 51-foot Wharram cat like his own Tehini for the same sort of sum you would pay for a 26-foot GRP production catamaran. Which is a thought worth thinking. It must be borne in mind, however, that the same 51-foot Wharram boat will have in effect not very much more accommodation than the smaller monocoque craft.

CHINE CONSTRUCTION

The third type of 'V' hull form is that employing chines. Here, only the underwater parts are 'Veed', and usually the 'V' is steep-sided forward, deepening to a considerable 'chest' just forward of amidships, before flattening out almost completely as it runs aft, to end under substantial, squarish transoms. The best known exponent of this shape, which is then presented above the chines with fairly upright, flared topsides, is of course Bill O'Brien.

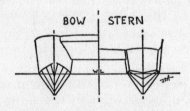

TYPICAL CHINE SECTIONS

His early Shamrock motor sailer of about 22 feet over-all was something of a trial piece for the enormously

popular eight-metre Bobcat, the impressive sales of which were largely organised by Tom and Mary Lack of Mudeford on Christchurch Harbour in Hampshire. Much of the type's popularity is undoubtedly due to the apparently inexhaustible efforts of these two enormously keen and good people, and their five equally enthusiastic sons. Between them, they organise all sorts of rallies and cruises-in-company, quite apart from running what must be one of the most active and happy Owners' Associations in the entire world of sailing.

The whole thing, I must emphasise, has been built upon the vision of Bill O'Brien, who, in the early days of catamarans, saw the possibility of providing really *comfortable* 'Mum, Dad, and the kids' cruising. He saw, in the double-canoe concept, the possibility of permanently made-up bunks which did not have to be converted into settees during the day, because there was ample room for proper settees as well. He saw the possibilities of wide, wide cockpits, where Gran could sit and enjoy the sun and sea air without everyone having to pardon their way round her in order to work the ship. He saw the value (and the attraction) of a long, luxurious galley with lots of draining board and 'working top' and masses of locker space, instead of the old single burner and washing-up bowl which yachtsmen had for generations passed off as 'the galley' in thousands of boats before. And he saw the possibility of something which was really safe at sea, by nature of its width and easy motion, so long as it hadn't a big enough rig to endanger it in a blow. And that just about describes the average Bobcat.

But we are supposed to be looking at hull forms, not people, and the principal behind this 'varying V' form, are firstly those of safety, coupled with fairly cheap construction. Several people have built their own Bobcats, though obviously the introduction of chines and the many alterations of angle between the bottom panels and the topsides makes this a more complicated job than, for instance, the tackling of a Wharram hull.

From the safety point of view, like Jim Wharram, Bill O'Brien has tended to avoid fixed keels or drop-keels projecting down below the natural line of the well-rockered hulls, because of the tripping effect which arises when the boat is thrust suddenly sideways by wind or wave. True, some of his designs, such as the Oceanic, had fins which project at an angle from the inboard chine of each hull, and these help to reduce leeway while actively 'catching' the water in such a way as to help hold the weather hull down, his most recent designs have been used to experiment with the water-ballast keel described earlier.

Basically though, it is the actual shape of the 'V' in the hull sections forward which act as 'keels', in that this shape cannot very easily be thrust sideways through the water—so long as it remains more or less upright. The great thing is that should the craft ever be thrown upon her beam ends, as they used to say, the broad angle of the 'V' presents its lee side to the water at an angle approaching the horizontal, so that it has hardly *any* resistance to leeway when in that attitude. The boat can thus immediately slide sideways when hit by a sea.

This kind of hull gives a reasonable performance to windward in normal cruising conditions, but if not fitted with extra and deeper fins or plates, it is naturally not brilliant to windward in a badly disturbed sea.

'U'-SHAPED HULLS

The remaining hull form which is commonly used is the

'U'-sectioned hull. This, for the most of its length, has entirely round bilges. The bottom (underwater) parts are basically composed of a semi-circle, though in designs such as those by Macalpine-Downie, the 'U' flattens out somewhat aft, and the bow of course narrows to a fine 'V' at the waterline, so as to provide the necessary 'entry' to cut through the surface with least resistance.

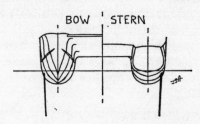

TYPICAL 'U' SECTIONS

It would seem from study of many race results that, taken all in all, this 'U' shape affords the highest overall performance, but with one very important limitation. A boat with this type of section below the waterline has very little natural reserve buoyancy compared, say, to a 'V' hull, so she simply *must* be kept as light as possible if her speed potential is to be realised. In other words, she's a poor load-carrier, in comparison to 'broad V' constructions.

The conclusion here is that if you want to race a lot, pick a catamaran with 'U' sections, and if you want her purely for comfortable cruising, choose one with underwater sections made up of some kind of fairly wide-angled 'V', but that is definitely not a 'hard and fast' rule. Against the fast 'U' shape is the fact that it in itself has so little resistance to leeway that some kind of extra keel form is essential for progress to windward. And there can be no doubt nowadays that with suitable keels or plates correctly shaped and positioned, such catamarans *can* be made to go to windward very smartly indeed, out-pointing and outsailing plenty of so-called 'fast' mono-hulls in the process.

If one can be bothered with drop-keels, no doubt these are the best and possibly the safest compromise, though only if they and their cases are *very* strongly constructed and fixed within the hulls. 'Safest', in this instance, in the sense that if crews know when and where *not* to use drop-keels, round-bilged boats can be made to behave very well at sea in either good or bad weather.

A cat with a deep drop-keel sticking down into dense water below her is less capable of 'riding a punch' than one without. The only sensible way to sail in squally weather where such knock-downs might occur through carrying too much sail, or because of exceptionally steep beam seas, is to raise the *lee* board completely, and use only the board in the *weather* hull to counteract leeway— unlike the barge-yacht tradition of using only the lee plate. Then, when the boat is hit by a really bad sea or squall, to the point of her weather hull lifting, the weather board lifts with it and to some extent 'spills' water, so letting the entire craft slide safely to leeward.

In practice, I am not convinced that even this tech-nique would work adequately or quickly enough to pre-vent a full capsize, but I will say more of this in the chapter on Handling Under Sail.

I am never happy with drop-keels of any kind. They can have problems when the boat is beached, in some cases, because stones tend to get trapped in the slots, and so on. If you ground accidentally with a board still down, it may be bent if of metal construction, and may then refuse to be lifted back up into its case, which in turn may make it impossible for the boat to be slipped for repairs.

Unless the boards are left down permanently, one has also the additional business of having to remember to operate them each time you get under way and moor up. And if you are as forgetful as I am you can find you have forgotten to raise or lower them, at an awkward time. Worse still; I know of so many toes (some of them mine) which have been broken on the drop-keel projections which tend to clutter already narrow-enough sidedecks, quite apart from the dangers there are of having one's feet slip on the ropes which operate the boards from the cockpit, and which therefore trail along the sidedecks in a most hazardous fashion. But I won't deny that drop-keels probably are the best way of obtaining really good windward performance.

WITH DAGGERS DRAWN...

The delightful little Hirondelle cat, with her truly astonishing performance, gets over some of the side-deck problem by employing dagger-boards instead of pivoted plates. This means a shorter slot for a start, but of course a partly raised board can present quite an obstacle for the unwary in a hurry to get forward! As a matter of interest, the Hirondelle also uses dagger-board rudder-blades, which seem to me a *far* better idea than the usual pivoted rudder-plate arrangement. Not only are the wooden boards lighter and easier to operate, but they can be used when half-raised in very shallow water without loss of rudder-balance, or fear of bending the plate or damaging the casing in the rudder stock, which are the main snags with half-raised pivoted blades.

People sometimes fret about the fact that dagger-boards will not swivel up when the boat runs aground or hits something. I may be wrong, but any time I put *Twintail* aground when her drop-keels were lowered, they never swung up on their own. There was always so much sideways pressure on them from the sails that they could not shift. So dagger-boards would appear to have hardly any disadvantage here.

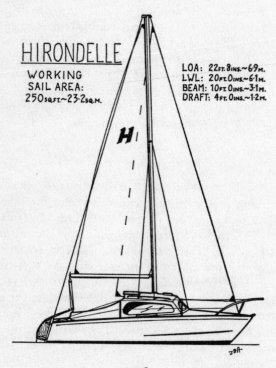

HIRONDELLE

WORKING
SAIL AREA:
250 sq.ft.~23·2 sq.m.

LOA: 22 ft. 8 ins.~6·9 m.
LWL: 20 ft. 0 ins.~6·1 m.
BEAM: 10 ft. 0 ins.~3·1 m.
DRAFT: 4 ft. 0 ins.~1·2 m.

Any kind of drop-keel has, however, one drawback which is very hard indeed to overcome—particularly if the cases have been made wide to allow for trapped stones, or even shaped to get extra 'lift' when beating to windward. Noise. I have yet to meet the drop-keel which does not thump or bump, or vibrate at speed, or generally produce some kind of intermittent noise, especially if a bit of a sea is running—and this can make life, particularly for anyone below and maybe trying to sleep, very tiresome!

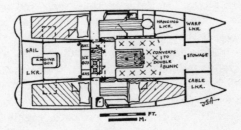

HIRONDELLE. Designed by C. Hammond; sold by Colin Kennedy Yacht Agency, 6 Nelson Place, Lymington, Hampshire, England. (Export only: Pennington Yachts, 11 Stem Lane Industrial Estate, New Milton, Hampshire, England.) GRP construction, with some balsawood sandwich. Lifting daggerboard keels and rudderblades. Tiller steering. Outboard motor in cockpit well. Sleeps 3/5. Twin companion hatches.

A small cruising cat with astonishingly high performance. Perhaps more suitable for coastal work than off-shore passages.

FLOTSAM TRAP

To go back for a minute to the idea of having a centrally mounted drop-keel slung beneath the bridgedeck. Apart from the strains which such a long projection must have on its connections, there is one thing which bothers me about *anything* normally projecting into the water between the hulls. (Outboard engines, for example.)

Because the two inboard bow-waves naturally tend to throw extra quantities of surface water inwards towards the centreline of a catamaran, they also tend to throw seaweed or any other flotsam there too. In my first Shearwater III racing cat, I found that often and again the centrally mounted dagger-board (which was both vast *and* heavy) had to be lifted up clear of the water to do away with some entanglement of bladder-wrack and other marine and man-made curiosities which perpetually gathered against its sharpish leading edge. And on countless flat calm passages at sea in *Twintail* I remember having to stop and tilt the outboard engine clear of accumulated vegetation—not to mention polythene bags and other flexible articles. Our outboard-powered Catalac suffers similar inconvenience from time to time.

For these reasons I have reservations about centrally mounted keels in particular, since they do tend to be in the water (in a sailing boat) even more frequently than the outboard engine, and if they are ballasted, it is going to be a considerable job to raise and clear them—once you have peered over the front to see if that is in fact what is slowing you up!

FIXED KEELS

Clearly the only alternative to drop-keels when something

simply has to be added to stop a particular hull making
leeway, is a pair of fixed and permanent keels of some
kind. Which brings us back to *Misty Miller*, and her
troubles. Her keels, which sheered off, one by one, were
of relatively high-aspect-ratio: deep and narrow.

From my own experience with drop-keels, not only on
little racing cats, but in our old Ranger 27 as well, the
pressure on them, when sailing at any reasonable speed
with the wind on or ahead of the beam, nearly always
prevented any attempts of mine to raise or lower them
with anything like ease. The difficulty was one of leverage.
The deeper the keel, the more the strain on hull and/or
plate case. With fixed keels, the danger point lies where
these are bolted to the hull, or even moulded on, come
to that, since obviously any breakage there is likely to
let in water.

If, however, you make use of long, *shallow* fixed keels
(low-aspect-ratio) instead of the supposedly more efficient
deep kind, the leverage on the hull where the two things
meet is going not only to be tiny by comparison, but
the 'join' itself is spread over a long distance and is
therefore much stronger anyway. Such keels also form a
grand base on which the boat can safely dry out, but
they can make her comparatively slow in stays.

Well then, why not have compromise keels, say, of
medium-aspect-ratio, not too shallow and not too short?
Simply because, the longer the keel (long fore-and-aft,
that is) the harder it is to 'stall' when working under
short canvas in bad weather, and because there is less of
the old 'tripping effect'. With a 'U' sectioned hull, a stub
of a keel not projecting more than a foot or so below
the bottom of the 'U' has very little grip of the water
if the boat is ever thrown up on her side by wind or
sea—which lets her slip away safely instead of holding

into the blow. So any advantage such a 'compromise keel' might have over the long, shallow variety is, to my way of thinking anyhow, outweighed at once by the lower stalling speed and greater safety factor of the latter.

SHARP PRACTICES

And now, bows. One sees every conceivable type of bow in use on catamarans. There are convex profiles, concave profiles, and even some attempts to copy the sixteenth-century artist William Hogarth's famous double-curved 'line of beauty'—a sort of abbreviated clipper-bow effect. One sees knife-like fineness carried from below the waterline almost all the way up to deck level, or straightforward curves, some without and some with 'knuckle' chines to add a bit of lift and keep some of the spray down. Then there are ordinary chines, tapering to nothing at the stem (as in Bobcats), and fine bows at waterlevel surmounted by widely flaring chines and broad, overhanging bows such as those on the Catalac.

So what are the effects of the different shapes? Once more, we have to decide what it is we each want from our particular boats. If one wishes for something which can slice through the seas and lose no speed when cutting into a short chop, no doubt the finely 'Veed' bow will do just that. But that kind has very little reserve buoyancy, and so is not well equipped to cope with all the forces of the rig thrusting it down. In some ways, therefore, it is not all that ideal for a boat which is likely to be repeatedly hard-driven.

A convex profile is better than a concave one, for it does offer something in the way of a reserve lift just above the normal waterline. If you could couple that with some adequate kind of knuckle-chine, broadening the bow without making it too full, then you would have a very fast bow indeed, and it is this which Macalpine-Downie has applied to his latest boats—with excellent results. The Prout brothers' Snowgoose 34 is also blessed with a form like this, though there they have given the top of the profile a concave turn which allows a broader forepeak deck, and just that edge of extra reserve buoyancy at the last minute, so to speak.

The hard-chine form of construction in itself leads to a natural chine bow which is just about perfect, so long as there is not too much fullness at the waterline. This is a bit hard to avoid when building in plywood, but easy enough in glass-reinforced plastic.

FINE, FLARING AND FULL BOWS

A logical development of this is seen in the Catalac bow, as it happens, in that she has fine waterlines right forward, closely surmounted by very broad, flaring chines, and topsides swept out from well-raked stems which are very full indeed. Not perhaps the best bow from a racing point of view, for she has a lot of freeboard forward, but grand for cruising purposes. The very fullness of the bows, while they provide a terrific safety margin against bow-depression, also slow her up somewhat when punching into a biggish head-sea. The racing boys would frown at that. But cruising folk usually have just a little more time on their hands, and are unlikely to mind a small drawback of this kind, especially when they appreciate the amount of safety which such a bow affords.

From the safety angle alone, a bow which prevents the rest of the boat from tripping herself up, is maybe what one should strive for in a cruising boat. Something very full, with lots of freeboard. Or so one might think. But freeboard means windage—which slows you up when beating (though not when reaching or running), and a full bow—the sort of thing they used to call a 'spoon' bow—would give her nothing to trip on at all, and furthermore would help her to ride up over the water when hard-pressed. Or (again) so one might think. But it's no good. A bow which is full at the waterline is *deadly* slow unless it is driven right up to planing speeds, when it is really quite good. But the trouble is getting it there. The drag of such a bow at moderate speeds turns out to be quite appalling—so one is well nigh *forced* to have narrow, fine waterlines anyway.

BULBOUS BOWS

One idea which I have yet to see applied to catamarans is that employed in most modern cargo ships nowadays —that bulbous underwater nose thing. I imagine this might be a most effective method of getting buoyancy right forward in the boat without reducing performance, but I have no way of knowing whether or not there may be reasons why it might not work. Certainly, when a boat so fitted pitches into a big steep sea, the 'bulb' will be brought out of the water, or at least up to the surface, far too frequently. Against that it can be argued that large merchantmen often pitch their 'big noses' out in a long swell, yet designers still produce them with this feature, so surely the advantages must outweigh the snags? Or is it all just a fashion?

THE END OF THE PROBLEM

In fact, as many a naval architect discovered long, long ago, it is the *stern* of a boat which tends to have most effect on her speed—the bow is merely a means of providing a suitable flow of water to course under the stern.

The tea clipper *Cutty Sark* was almost designed round her stern, and it was that which enabled her to out-run far longer (and so, one would think, far faster) ships in the wild Indian Ocean. In those conditions, pooping was the big danger. *Cutty Sark* was given a stern which helped to avoid pooping, so that she could run on at speed long after most other vessels had been forced to shorten sail for safety.

Catamarans do not normally suffer from being pooped, unlike conventional monohulled yachts, so that is not the sort of stern one necessarily needs. Just let us think exactly what it is one *does* want.

DESIGN FOR THE RIGHT CONDITIONS

Most family sailing—indeed most pleasure boating, which should come to the same thing—is done in light conditions. Nice day, sparkling sun, light breeze allowing one to carry reasonably large sails without putting a strain on anything, yet giving the boat good speed. It doesn't actually happen *just* like that terribly often; not in British waters, anyway. But that is what we *like*, and what draws us to the water more than any other set of conditions.

Catamarans are supposed to be fast boats. That is undoubtedly a case for giving them the sort of stern which performs at its best when the boat is hard-driven and going like mad. But how often in the course of a season's sailing does one in fact come across the exact circumstances when the boat *can* meet her ideal and fly along at top speed? Not only does the wind have to be just the right strength, but the sea has to be right too.

And more important still, one's course over the water has to be at just the right angle to the wind in order to extract that Peak Performance of which she is only then capable.

WATER BARRIER?

Now, it takes quite a weight of wind to get the average 26- to 36-foot (say, 8- to 11-metre) cat up over a curious 'barrier' which comes into play at around the eight-knot mark, and reaches its upper limit at about ten knots. Up to probably $7\frac{1}{2}$ knots the catamaran behaves much like any other sailing craft in many respects. Between eight and ten there is this strange time when it seems to take either the back of a good long sea for her to surf down, or a very considerable increase in wind-strength to get her going any faster. Then all of a sudden she's 'through', and flying off at a great pace; twelve, fifteen knots or far more (depending on the boat), with a distinct feeling that she has somehow reduced friction and is roaring along on a pair of rails, helter-skelter down a superb, never-ending hill. It is something like planing in a racing dinghy or powerboat, but isn't quite that, as I understand it.

However, when this 'thing' happens, it is a comparatively rare occasion, in a family cruising boat anyhow. Pottering along in gentle sunshine and a pleasant breeze is much more commonly the case (says he, blissfully ignoring quite purposely the horrid-wet-cold-blowing days which inevitably plague us between times!). But mainly when cruising, if it is a really nasty day with strong winds, one does tend to stay in port if possible, on the off-chance that tomorrow will be nicer and we can all go sailing again.

The trouble is, the sort of catamaran stern which is

best for the hard winds and high-speed stuff, is absolutely useless when it comes to slow, peaceful sailing in anything less than Force 4 or so. And the statistics show all too clearly that *then* is undoubtedly when most of us do practically all our sailing—Force 4 or less. So why in the world give a catamaran (or any boat) the sort of stern that is *only* good when it's blowing harder than that? You may well ask! Yet many, many well-known designs do indeed have the sort of 'fast' transom sterns which drag in the water at slow speeds, slowing the boat even more.

WHAT SHAPE OF STERN?

What most cruising people probably want is the sort of stern which has the very minimum of drag at the bottom range of speeds. Not only will they then make faster passages in those nice light conditions, but the boat will all the quicker be capable of coming up to those super-eight-knot bursts which we all revel in and love to brag about.

Take as an example, the early Prout designs. Most of these had 'U' shaped transoms which performed superbly at speed, but which dragged quite atrociously, not to say deafeningly, at low speeds. 'Pulling half the ocean astern of them', as someone unkindly put it. Fortunately Roland and Francis Prout are never given to much standing still, and the four-foot extension to the Ranger 27 sterns (which made the same boat into a Ranger 31) was a cheap and quick attempt to get over the immediate problem. It of course left the boat rather narrow for her length, and she still had transoms, albeit small ones. In certain seas, even they still dipped and dragged. The 45-foot Ocean Ranger, which was the Prouts' next design for production, was for this reason given taller, narrower transoms, which in the normal way do not drag much at low speeds. But the conclusion to all this came when they designed the very advanced Snowgoose 34.

Snowgoose 34 goes the whole hog, as they say, in many ways. Where her sterns are concerned, she is particularly unusual, for she has no transoms at all, and no real stern-posts either, come to that. Instead, the tail of each hull is tapered away to fair exactly into a thick, moulded rudder-blade, which naturally tapers away to nothing.

The result is interesting in two ways. There is absolutely the very minimum possible drag at low speed, with the effect that she only very seldom seems to sail at what could be called 'low speeds', and secondly, there is very little resistance to pitching. So one thing is good, and the other not so good. However, while this kind of stern will allow the vessel to pitch readily, the pitching itself hardly seems to take any speed off her, the way it inevitably must with a transom-sterned craft.

Overhung sterns, as such, are not quite the thing in catamarans, because it is generally agreed that transoms are best at high speed. Yet canoe-type sterns, like narrowly 'Veed' bows, present too little resistance to pitching for many folk's taste. John Winterbotham of M.G. Duff & Partners, in designing the hull lines of the nine-metre Catalac, came up with what I find a very acceptable answer. He gave his hulls a broad, powerful pair of sterns, under which the 'V' hull sections have been progressively flattened out almost completely as they come aft; much as in many Bill O'Brien designs. But where Winterbotham has scored, in my opinion, is that the almost square transoms with which the hulls terminate are carried well clear above the water, and remain clear even when the craft is heavily laden.

This arrangement gives an exceptionally buoyant stern, highly resistant to pitching (which matches well the broad chines and flaring sections forward), yet which has the minimum drag at low speeds. She has, in fact, that old and well-tried combination which amongst East Coast fishermen in the 'days of sail' used to be referred to as a 'cod's head and a mackerel's tail', so far as her underwater shape is concerned. Her long, flat run aft gives her truly vivid downwind performance, and in Force 2, speeds in excess of five and six knots seem normal enough, even close-hauled. But a lot of designers prefer other shapes, and even other rudders hung in other places.

RUDDER EFFICIENCY

I have discussed the angles at which rudders are best set in the chapter on capsizing—those situated so that the heel of the stock is *ahead* of the rudderhead, so that when the helm is put over at speed the flow of water across the blade is angled if anything upwards to help hold the stern down and the bows up.

A further, obvious point is that any kind of rudder which is hung on the very tail of the boat is easier to maintain than one hung under an overhanging stern and operated through a tubular gland. The tail-end rudder may also be of the lifting variety, whereas the kind hung further forward under the hull cannot readily have this facility.

The under-hull position, however, does tend to be more efficient in many ways—it is less likely to come clear of the water in a short choppy sea or on a steeply breaking ocean crest, and generally it works in a denser flow of water where there is less chance of cavitation spoiling the flow round it.

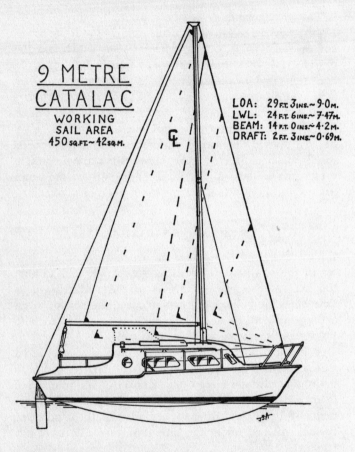

9 METRE
CATALAC
WORKING
SAIL AREA
450 SQ.FT.~ 42 SQ.M.

LOA: 29 FT. 3 INS.~ 9·0 M.
LWL: 24 FT. 6 INS.~ 7·47 M.
BEAM: 14 FT. 0 INS.~ 4·2 M.
DRAFT: 2 FT. 3 INS.~ 0·69 M.

Any form of fixed rudder, when fitted to a craft like a catamaran which is quite likely to be allowed to take the ground now and then on her own bottoms, should of course be protected by some kind of fixed fin or skeg immediately forward of the blade. But even then, if the bottom of the hulls is heavily rockered or sloped, it is

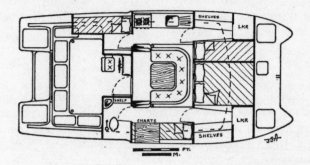

CATALAC. Designed by J. Winterbotham and T. M. Lack; sold by Tom Lack Catamarans Ltd., Avon Works, Bridge Street, Christchurch, Hampshire, England. GRP construction. No keels, relies on hull shape to reduce leeway. Lifting rudderblades. Wheel steering. Outboard motor or twin petrol inboard installations. Sleeps 5 comfortably, in four separate cabins. Room for more in saloon. Spacious accommodation suitable for extended cruises. Sheltered steering position.

A comfortable all-out cruising boat, reasonable to windward, but with exceptional downwind performance. Good in light airs. An able seaboat.

more than just likely that when she dries out on mud or something fairly soft, the skegs *and* the rudder-blades will tend to dig in, if they have much weight to carry. There is then the danger of maybe a differently-directioned tidal current, or perhaps a new and strong wind direction, causing the boat to swing suddenly round as she floats off again. If the rudders are then held by the mud, they might well be damaged.

And that is why I am prepared in my own catamaran to put up with transom-hung lifting rudders, even though

151

(just as with drop-keels) they constitute another couple of things one has to remember to do before the yacht can be got under way.

I have now talked about hull centre-sections, bows, and about sterns. I have not more than briefly mentioned pitching, as part of the average catamaran's motion at sea. Unfortunately, while catamarans will heel ('roll', if you must have it that way) only about eight degrees even in strong winds, most of them will try to emulate rocking horses in anything of a head-sea.

Pitching, where one has two slim hulls acting as a unit, is a problem. It happens readily, simply because catamarans usually carry a largish rig for the sort of reserve buoyancy which their necessarily fine ends are capable of providing. The narrower and finer the ends, the worse the pitching, to make a singularly sweeping statement. (Not quite true, either, but that's the general theory.) Sharp, knife-like bows do nothing to help, neither do 'U'-shaped transoms unless they are very flattened and broad indeed. Jim Wharram's feeling that if one end of a hull closely matches the shape of the other, any attempt to pitch is naturally damped out by equal and opposing forces, only seems in practice to work out some of the time, depending on the state of the seas and also the rig, which provides the forward thrusts and leverage which helps to start a boat plunging.

So, either you design a hull which doesn't *mind* pitching and is not going to be slowed up by it more than a little, such as the Prout Snowgoose 34, Wharram's Polynesian Cats, and the grand little Heavenly Twins 26-footer, or you design hulls which are as highly resistant as possible to pitching, such as those by O'Brien and others, incorporating pronounced chines and broad transoms, just above the waterlines.

The Tom Lack/John Winterbotham Catalac uses this method to some advantage, as I have already explained.

LOW-SLUNG BRIDGEDECKS

There is one other way of stopping pitching, though I am not very keen on it. What you have to do is have a fairly low bridgedeck carried well forward and well aft. Early cruising catamarans often had such an arrangement, notably the smaller Prout boats, some early Henderson designs, and more recently the big twelve-metre Solaris luxury cat. The trouble here is the considerable noise and often vicious jolting and banging which can be caused by seas striking the underside of the thing. This can be hard on crews' nerves, crockery, and anyone trying to sleep.

There is also a noticeable amount of drag generated by the bridgedeck's repeated contact with wave-tops. All the same, when it does come slamming down as the boat pitches, it stops her at once from going any further once it has 'bottomed', and in reducing risk of a nose-dive, it could be said to have a bearing on safety, though such an arrangement must put considerable strain on the very best of structures. Not that in all the years we owned her was there the slightest sign of damage in that connection to our Ranger 27.

One recent design which was deliberately given a low bridgedeck for safety reasons is the Heavenly Twins centre cockpit double-ender by Pat Patterson. But he, like the Prouts in their 34-footer, gets over the slam problem by using a central longitudinal 'pod' running down the length of the bridgedeck itself, and so shaped as to 'skwudge' rather than slam through those crests which it comes across.

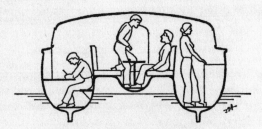

HOW REASONABLE HEADROOM CAN BE
ACHIEVED EVEN ON A SHORT, 21ft.6in.
(6·5m.) W.L. LENGTH – AS IN
HEAVENLY TWINS

In any event, it seems that if any sailing boat is to be driven hard to windward, her construction should be especially strong in the region around a position three-tenths of her maximum waterline length aft from the bow waterline. For it is here—in almost any craft—where the worst pounding, and what might be termed 'squeezing', happens.

I have watched many catamaran hulls 'panting' in and out at this point as the boat slices into a sea. The pounding point, for want of a better term, on a bridgedeck above water level, is of course just a trifle further aft, so if a cat can be provided with a bulkhead, partial bulkhead, or other reinforcement at this general area, so much the better.

Anyway, from the performance and certainly from the comfort point of view, it would seem that bridgedecks should be kept as high off the water as they can be. But unless one is to put up with a towering, multistepped superstructure, as in some of Bill O'Brien's motor-sailer cats, which have a kind of 'doghouse' over the saloon area, headroom on the bridgedeck is going to be low.

BRIDGEDECK HEADROOM

Sufficient headroom to permit comfortable seating round the cabin table is of course possible without the boat looking like a floating caravan, but to provide more than just that and at the same time keep the profile low, either means low clearance beneath the bridgedeck, or some kind of foot-well. The 22-foot Hirondelle has just such a well projecting down under the site of her cabin table, in order to provide knee-room for diners. The 26-foot Heavenly Twins uses a long 'pod' for partly the same reason, and the Prout brothers before that developed the idea born originally in the mind of Colin Mudie, and fitted their Snowgoose 34 with a carefully shaped pod or 'nacelle' as they call it. (Colin Mudie first tried this out on a floatable balloon gondola, if my memory serves me right, and then used the same idea to house the engine in Dr Lewis's 45-foot Prout-built catamaran *Rehu Moana*.)

Such nacelles or pods, call 'em what you will, provide excellent headroom below decks, though crossing from one hull right over to the other in boats so designed means climbing up, across, down, across, up, across, and down into the hull, which no doubt one gets used to in time! A major advantage, however, is that the auxiliary engine may be housed in the pod, and the propeller lowered into the water well forward, which does go far towards reducing cavitation problems, of which more anon. Moreover, because of the shape of such projections, bridgedeck slamming is almost eliminated. The fact that the wave-tops do surge along the pod's under side seems to matter very little indeed.

If most of this chapter has been taken up with shape and its effects, it is because to my way of thinking the right shape, properly constructed, is going to have more bearing on the boat's general qualities than good construction of the wrong shape. No boat-builder worth his salt is going to turn out an inadequately constructed boat if he can possibly help it, so what the customer must most concern himself with in the first place is the design of the boat rather than how she is put together. It is the job of the designer to make sure that the builder does his work properly on whatever shape the boat happens to be—no matter what appropriate material has been chosen for her construction.

But a brief glance at some of the methods of construction is worth while, all the same.

Wood is still largely considered as the best boat-building material, though where multihulls are concerned and lightweight strength is at a premium, some form of plywood is the normal thing. Cold moulding techniques, where strips of ply or veneers are glued together in at least two directions, layer upon layer over a male mould, is not only light, but immensely strong, and as a rule is easily maintained as well. There will, as with any form of construction, be the usual need for internal reinforcing with stringers, bulkheads and so on. The trouble is that wood has recently become increasingly expensive, and shows every sign of being classed (and priced) as a luxury before very long.

156

Aluminium is another suitable material, though dirty to work with. Several large catamarans have been built this way, the various parts being joined together by argon-arc welding. A very pleasing result can thus be obtained, though as with other metals, if the hull is dented by contact with an obstruction (to put it nicely), the dent may be permanent unless major work is carried out.

Steel is another possibility, though until some really rust-resistant steel is available at a sensible cost (a thing called Copper Varium Steel looks like being a possibility), steel hulls have of necessity to be heavily constructed in order to allow for corrosion. And catamarans must be kept light if they are to be at all successful.

Ferro-Cement or Reinforced Concrete has been tried with most shapes of boat, and with most shapes of boat it is successful enough. Amateurs can build with it and achieve good results with practice, but again, where catamarans are concerned, the need to keep the craft as light as possible means the thinnest possible application and reinforcing, which is neither easy to achieve nor a particularly good idea when stresses of the nature suffered by most multihulled yachts are concerned.

Then there is the full gamut of *plastics*, from the wide range of ordinary glass-reinforced plastics using chopped-strand and/or woven glass cloth and resin, to those sandwiching balsawood blocks or other foam fillings. The most popular method at the time of writing is still the former, such boats as the Catalac, Hirdondelle, Snowgoose 34 being among those using 'solid' GRP. The Macalpine-Downie designs built by Seacraft of Brightlingsea, Essex, including the popular Iroquois and Cherokee cats, have always been turned out in a sandwich construction encapsulating blocks of balsawood between the resin-glass skins. This results in something which is extremely light, strong, and well insulated, which cuts down the condensation problems caused by 'solid' GRP. It also has the very great virtue of being in itself highly buoyant, so that additional built-in buoyancy is usually unnecessary.

Recently a product known as 'Unitex' foam has become available, and at first sight this looks very good indeed. Thermo-formed, and of high density if need be where tight curves are required, this stuff is intended specially for boat-building. It can be bent to shape readily, can be screwed together or tongued-and-grooved edge to edge, and the manufacturers supply a top-quality glue with the material. One can, apparently, cut it and alter it to the desired shape, or leave it flat. From the Do-It-Yourself point of view, material of this kind must bring many designs into the field of possibility—but the actual designer of the boat chosen would of course have to be carefully consulted before this (or *any* kind of construction other than that originally intended for the boat in question) is tried. I have no personal experience of 'Unitex' foam (made by Unitex Marine, Knaresborough, Yorkshire HG5 OPP), so I have no way of knowing if the above claims are in fact going to make boat-building as easy as it all sounds. The information came from an Amateur Yacht Research Society report, and from the makers of the material themselves. Anyone interested should contact them.

8

Sail Plans and Hull Balance

Just as hull shape in this light, unballasted and very shoal-draft type of craft is highly critical and important, so naturally are the rigs which go with them. Most rigs normally seen on monohulled yachts can be employed on a multihull, but it is not quite as straightforward as that.

I explained in earlier chapters how, when one has a long and shallow pair of hulls, the power-thrust of the rig is angled downwards over the lee bow most of the time, and because the lee bow is thereby somewhat depressed even a little, the CLR (Centre of Lateral Resistance) of the entire craft moves considerably forward —far more than it tends to in a monohull. As a result of this, the Centre of Elevation (the middle of the sail area) so to speak gets 'left behind', causing severe tendencies to luff if things are not previously organised so as to prevent the effect. Which in well designed catamarans, they of course are.

However, because of the tendency, *most catamarans behave poorly under main alone when beating*. They generally do far better under a reasonable-sized genoa foresail only, when one wishes to manoeuvre under just the one sail. The point this emphasises is that in catamarans, the headsail or forecanvas is what does most of the work.

It has long been known, even in single-hulled yachts, that a sail set behind a stay tends to be far more efficient than one set behind a mast, at least where windward work is concerned. Add to this what I have just said about catamarans, and it becomes clear that what is wanted for best efficiency on a cat is undoubtedly a 'large-headsail' rig, of some kind.

CATAMARAN RIGS

A perfectly normal, conventionally proportioned Bermudian sloop rig, where the mainsail is about the same size or slightly smaller than the fore-triangle, does work on a cat; but she will tend to become unbalanced in a freshening wind, and early reefing of the mainsail will be necessary, not so much because the boat is becoming over-driven, as simply because she is becoming impossible to hold on course. Even then, this rig *can* be used successfully, so long as the CE is kept well forward, in relation to the CLR. However, if the mast is stepped very much forward of amidships in a cat, downwind the boat tends to bury her noses, which again may cause her to gripe round.

It does not mean that a large mainsail, small headsail rig cannot be satisfactory on a cat. Pat Patterson's Heavenly Twins handles beautifully with just this arrangement, her hull having stub keels *and* skegs, mounted well aft to provide the proper balance.

In most catamarans however, a single-masted rig is best if the 'mainsail' is not over-large, so that most of the area can be carried in the headsail.

THE 'MINS'L' RIG

The varying proportions of such a rig can be carried to

surprising extremes with success—as has been proved by
the somewhat strange-looking arrangement adopted by
the Prouts for their excellent Snowgoose 34 catamaran.
It is basically a cutter rig, but the mast is shortish,
stepped well aft of amidships, and sports a truly tiny
'mainsail'—so tiny as to have been nicknamed the *mins'l*.
There is a low, and quite small foresail or staysail ahead
of that, which may be boomed or not as you wish, and
then the principal driving sail is, or rather are, a selection of vast jibs and genoas set on the long, sloping, masthead forestay. At this angle, they provide a certain
amount of 'lift', helping to keep the bows up, but also
giving the boat an exceptionally well-balanced high performance without any effort at all—it seems. (The sheet-
winches are well up to the job.) It all looks a bit peculiar,
but there can be no doubt whatever that for both racing
and cruising the 'Mins'l Rig' has already proved very
successful indeed.

TWO-STICKERS

So far as I am aware, there are no yawl-rigged catamarans, merely because catamarans are seldom given long
overhangs aft on which the mizzen mast might be stepped
abaft the line between the rudderheads.

Ketch rig, on the other hand, is fairly common. For
cruising, when one might often be under comfortably reduced sail in order, say, to work the ship into some
anchorage quietly without whizzing in at high speed in a
breeze and yet wishing to retain full manoeuvrability,
there is something to be said for this rig.

The mizzen, in that case, should be just large enough
to balance the headsails when the main is stowed, thus
giving the boat good control under all conditions. Un-

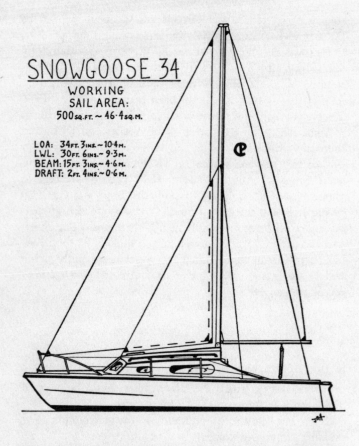

SNOWGOOSE 34

WORKING
SAIL AREA:
500 sq.ft. ~ 46·4 sq.m.

LOA: 34 ft. 3 ins. ~ 10·4 m.
LWL: 30 ft. 6 ins. ~ 9·3 m.
BEAM: 15 ft. 3 ins. ~ 4·6 m.
DRAFT: 2 ft. 4 ins. ~ 0·6 m.

fortunately, if the mizzen is large enough to be really useful as a driving sail, the windward performance of the craft is likely to be quite a lot worse than it would be with, say, a sloop or cutter rig. This is partly because of the old thing about sails behind masts being inefficient anyway, and partly because when working to windward a mizzen is almost always in the turbulent backwind

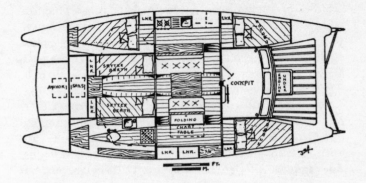

SNOWGOOSE 34. Designed by R. & F. Prout. Sold by Prout Catamarans, The Point, Canvey Island, Essex, England. GRP construction. Low aspect-ratio keels and fixed-draft rudders. Wheel steering. 25hp diesel mounted in central nacelle. Spacious accommodation with vast saloon where headroom is aided by the nacelle. 3 double berths and 3 singles.

A high performance cruiser of advanced design, luxuriously finished and easily handled. Successor to the Ranger 27 (31) and Ocean Ranger.

flowing off the mainsail—so it never does much work at all until the boat is eased away on a reach. Again, and even then, as the lee bow sinks slightly under the rig's thrust, and the CLR moves forward, one doesn't really want much sail set far aft in the boat.

A mizzen does of course provide something on which to hang a powerful reaching sail (how *did* such things become known as mizzen 'staysails', when they are invariably set flying?), but in my experience in an assortment of cruising ketches, the number of times the course and wind are just right for setting such a sail are few and far between.

However, there can be no doubt that for short-handed sailing in the larger catamarans (say, anything much over 36 feet or 11 metres in length) a two-masted rig is almost essential, and I can't see any advantage in giving a catamaran a schooner rig, since the biggest area is then in quite the least useful position.

One further two-masted rig, tried out in Prout's early *Ebb & Flo*, and again more recently in their much modified Ocean Ranger, *Yo*, steps a mast on each hull, each with its own sloop sail plan. When beating or reaching, one rig must interfere not a little with its neighbour, but downwind, with a special spinnaker set between the two goosewinged mainsails, it all comes into its own. But for cruising it must be rather hard work, what with two mainsails to set and stow.

TYPES OF SAIL

As far as the actual sails themselves are concerned, nearly everything has been tried with varying success, from Chinese lugsail mainsails, to gaff, gunter and Bermudian sails of either the fully-battened or 'soft', short-battened conventional kind. James Wharram has long favoured (I suspect partly because he likes the look of them) the cheap and simple spritsail rig for many of his designs. In short, nearly anything works—so long as the proportions and balance are right.

SIZE OF RIG

Most cruising men tend to find themselves short-handed, at least from time to time, and it is my belief that any cruising boat should be capable of being sailed single-handed anyway—just in case.

Racing folk are usually prepared to experiment with

the latest fashions if they are blessed with the right size of bank-roll, but the average cruising man merely wants the most suitable, easily handled rig which will give him a satisfactory performance both when passage-making, and when pottering in-shore amongst a crowd of other craft, or up some winding creek or sea loch. For him, ketch rig is one answer, though in cats under ten metres there is little doubt that a single-masted rig is really more efficient. (And cheaper.)

While the cruising owner may not be much bothered about getting the last degree of high-pointing and fast-footing when close-hauled, I think it is worth remembering that relatively few real cruising catamarans are faster to windward than monohulls of the same length—therefore if they are given rigs which do not perform well on the wind, they are likely to be quite poor to windward, which most people find unsatisfactory.

At the same time, it can be argued that since catamarans are relatively fast boats downwind, it is therefore sensible to give them a rig suitable mainly for downwind sailing, so as to take proper advantage of her best qualities. I personally feel that whereas that might indeed be the best thing to do if long ocean passages are contemplated, anyone who has done much coastal cruising will know the value of a weatherly craft, and for that reason a catamaran intended for coastal work should at least be given a reasonably weatherly rig. She will still go well enough to satisfy anyone downwind, so long as enough canvas can be added in the way of large headsails.

Spinnakers, because of the wide foredecks and steady platform which the crews of catamarans can enjoy, hold few of the horrors which one suffers from them in mono-hulls, and of course the setting of twin headsails presents no problems at all.

This all amounts to saying that, for best all-round cruising performance, it would seem that some kind of single-masted Bermudian rig, be it sloop, cutter or 'mins'l', is best for the smaller range of catamaran, and a small-mizzened ketch rig ideal for the larger ones. But it's all a matter of personal preferences, of course, *and* what is currently available!

NEED FOR CONSTANTLY SET HEADSAILS

There is one feature which I wish to stress, however, regarding headsails. Very few catamarans are happy under main alone, as I have explained. Being so light, they do not carry their way long enough to be sure of tacking reliably without a headsail set. Indeed many will in anything of a sea try to turn up head-to-wind whether the helmsman wishes it or not, just as soon as the headsail is taken off her. For this reason, changing headsails is best done very rapidly and efficiently, or, at best, a lot of speed will be lost.

There is another reason why quick changing of headsails is specially important in a catamaran. As already stated, it is the headsail which is the most powerful sail in a cat; therefore the boat will only go really well with the biggest possible headsail set, suitable to the conditions of wind and sea at any given moment. Which is all very well.

The trouble is, as any experienced catamariner will know, that whereas a monohull will lie down and spill wind off the top of her sails if she is suddenly over-pressed by an unexpected squall, the catamaran will not, or rather *should not* be allowed to heel. She won't *want* to anyway, unless you really have overdone things! But unless one is going to rely on automatic sheet release gear, or the quickness of the crew in letting sheets fly, one quite often finds that the necessity to change to a smaller headsail arrives without much warning—and it might not be convenient either to go reaching off to leeward, or to have the boat weathercock if she will not sail close-hauled under her mainsail, while the genoa is lowered and a smaller jib hanked on and hoisted and sheeted home in its place.

ROLLER-REEFING JIBS

There are several answers to the problem. One is to buy a set of 'Sailchangers' (or whatever they might be called) —devices which 'cartridge-load' the hanks on to the stay in one movement, so as to save time. But that will still leave you for a short time without any head-canvas set.

Another way is to have a really good, strong, reliable roller-headsail arrangement, so that the sail can be reefed to whatever area seems just right, at the pull of a furling line. Maybe that is the best answer, in that it is both instant and may be variable to the last degree. But rolling can never be good for a sail; the shape of its edges is bound to suffer. And unless the whole thing is always lowered when the boat is left at her moorings, the exposed edges of the rolled up sail will eventually rot from sunlight.

Even more important: The engineering of the roller gear must be absolutely right, so as to be capable of working properly under the extreme conditions of loading which a multihull can impose on her rigging. However, if one can be satisfied that it *will* work every time, and will not let down its owner or its mast, then of course it should all cost slightly less than a full set of fore-and-aft headsails, even when one includes the cost of a spare emergency headsail, in case the other one rips. Both sails will of course have to be cut to suit, so that the sheeting point will not alter as the sail is rolled.

TWIN FORESTAYS—AN EXCELLENT ANSWER

If you buy a cat which has only the one forestay and is possessed of, say, three different headsails already, a better answer may be to convert her to a twin-forestay system. All that is needed is either a double fitting on the deck, the lugs or tangs of which should preferably be at least four inches (about ten cm) apart, though I have found that $3\frac{1}{2}$ inches will just about do on a boat under thirty foot overall. To these the forestay rigging-screws are attached, and the stays lead parallel up to either a double tang at the masthead, or to a triangular steel plate of adequate strength, hung from the existing tang. The thing is to keep the stays apart all the way up.

A second jib halyard will be needed, and this is best not hung from the spinnaker crane, so maybe a block will have to be installed elsewhere. In my own boat I have a central hole for the second halyard block in the triangular spreading plate at the masthead, between the two stays, as it were. This helps divide the strain when a sail is hoisted on that halyard, rather than on the one she was originally fitted with, which in her case leads through a masthead sheave.

Since all our headsails, other than the huge ghoster, were in any case designed to sheet to the same point on deck, the one pair of sheets do most of the work. To change jibs, we simply use a 'lazy sheet' (consisting of a single rope with a snap-hook at one end), and start by clipping it into the clew of the in-use sail and bowsing it down to a convenient cleat, so that the proper sheets can be unclipped and attached to the new sail, which is now hanked on to the second forestay. With halyard and tack ready, the new sail is then hoisted alongside the in-use one (it makes little difference whether it goes up to windward or to leeward). Once the new sail is set and sheeted home with the working sheets, the old sail can be lowered. In this way the boat is at no time without a headsail properly sheeted and drawing, so no speed or control is lost.

If the skipper suspects a change in wind-strength, the appropriate sail can be made ready in plenty of time, and used or not as things turn out. But without having a suitable roller-reefing gear, I can see no other way of ensuring that the boat has a headsail working all the time.

So, ideally, either one chooses a catamaran with cutter rig (so that at least a foresail is set while you change jibs), or you have a roller system or a twin forestay set-up complete with duplicate halyards, (whic will help enormously when is comes to setting twin headsails rather than a spinnaker when running).

Many, many cats are sloop rigged with just the one forestay and jib halyard, and presumably their owners don't mind. But for catamaran sailing in squally coastal areas, or in confined waters, some quick method of altering headsail area is a most valuable asset.

9

Handling Under Sail

I have already spoken of some of the various handling peculiarities of catamarans under sail ... There is the effect of thrust on or over the lee bow, and the way that in turn can effect the steering. There is the need I outlined above which most catamarans have, of requiring a headsail to be set and drawing practically full time. But I think that once one understands and appreciates the fact that *unballasted, high-windage craft like catamarans do not carry their way more than a length or two* when the sheets are let fly or the sail is allowed to flap, then one is half way to knowing how to handle them.

All it really means is that you have to keep a catamaran really sailing at all times. Pinching up that last bit to windward is a fool's game in a cat. Starve her sails and she'll sag away to leeward at a great rate. Sail her good and full, especially in a sea, and she'll foot fast and make well to weather.

In a catamaran there can be no rounding up into the wind and 'shooting' through a gap between moored boats, or anything like that. If the gap cannot be made with the sails trimmed and full of wind, then one must *not* attempt it under sail alone—in any unballasted multihull, come to that. If you starve the sails, you kill the cat! And if the wind stops, the boat stops. Yet, on the other hand, as soon as the sails fill, your catamaran is off, accelerating forwards at once, using every puff fully.

REVERSING UNDER SAIL

Another advantage is that most catamarans can be made to reverse downwind very precisely under sail, without any great tendency to pay off unless the helm is put over—and there are occasions when that can be most useful in clearing a crowded anchorage, for instance.

TACKING, AND ALL THAT

Most people know that some early catamarans were not always very good at tacking, though more recent boats come round with the reliability of a racing dinghy. But even with them it must be remembered that just as with many small single-hulled cruisers, there are times, as in a jump of a sea for instance, when it will be necessary to let the jib back momentarily when tacking, just to help her head through the wind's eye. The early cats would frequently refuse to come about at all unless this was done as a matter of course, and many catamariners have developed the habit of doing it anyway, even in their more modern and much handier craft.

Tacking *is* just a little different in a cat than in ballasted craft, and the general principle is this:

Just before tacking, when anything of a sea is running, it may be advisable to let her pay off briefly, so as to ensure that she has plenty of way on. The helm is then eased firmly over, increasingly smartly as she comes round—and it must be *held* over until the sails have properly filled on the new tack. As she comes up into the wind, whereas in a monohull one could normally let go the lee jib sheet, in many catamarans it pays to hold it in, just until it has back-filled and no more.

The moment her head is actually through the eye of the wind, the headsail may be brought across and sheeted in as quickly as possible. There are still some older cats about which, if the headsail is not sheeted smartly, will start to weathercock under the pressure of the mainsail even though the helm may be hard over, but happily most recent designs have overcome this trait.

Again, some catamarans may tend to 'fall off before the wind' immediately after tacking, especially in light going, simply because their light weight has not enabled them to carry steerage way right through the tack. But whereas in a monohull this behaviour would be embarrassing, not to say extremely awkward, it matters not at all in a cat (even though it may look odd to a bystander), for as soon as the sails begin to draw, she is under control and sailing.

Some very early cats may even make something of a sternboard after tacking. My old *Twintail* used to do so occasionally, particularly if I had been pinching her just before putting the helm down. It never mattered, though, because a second or two of reversed helm would reliably force her to pay off on the desired tack. I soon learnt to allow a bit of elbow room when tacking, just in case this should happen. Part of her trouble was that she lacked the deep 'chest' in her underwater profile which most later designs have been given, and therefore she had immense directional stability. By the time she had come round on to a new tack, she was naturally prone to lose steerage-way. Even so, in seven years of cruising in her, it never got us into any kind of trouble, simply because of her typical catamaran ability to get going again practically instantly. As I say, most modern designs usually tack with utter confidence.

MANOEUVRING UNDER HEADSAIL ONLY

When working into an anchorage under sail in a sloop rigged catamaran it generally proves better to come in under headsail only, rather than the main only, in that with a reasonable size of headsail she will tack confidently. And with only a mains'l set, she probably won't. Under just a headsail, if the wind falls light in the lee of some big ship or building, for instance, and it is then necessary to tack, one should allow for the fact that her bows might blow off to leeward a little if she loses steerage way.

Tacking under mainsail alone is a different matter. Some cats do it well enough, though most of them do not like the manoeuvre at all. In any event it is better, bearing in mind the lack of momentum, to sail pretty free when under main only. Do not try to point up too high, and keep plenty of way on all the time. Then, when the helm is put over, the cat will swing rapidly up head-to, and should pay off without too much difficulty. With any shortage of steerage way, however, it is not hard to see that there will be quite a tendency under after canvas alone to turn back up head to wind as soon as the sail fills, so the rudders *must* be kept over until she answers them and is steering properly. It may in some boats prove necessary to release the mainsheet during a 'main-only' tack, and deliberately let her pay right off on to a reach before attempting to get her sailing close-hauled again.

DOWNWIND SLEDGING

Downwind there is rarely any problem with a catamaran. She will sledge along, bolt upright and steady, and all the fears of unexpected gybes when on a dead run, which those of us brought up in monohulls have ingrained in our souls, may largely be forgotten—for three reasons.

Catamarans do not roll (at all) downwind—unless there is a cross-sea—so there is less swaying of the main-sail to force a gybe. Its leech is not thrown about, and the boom is steady.

Catamarans tend to run straight and true—yawing does not occur except as a result of the helm being fiddled with, therefore again the wind is less likely to get the wrong side of the sail unintentionally.

And finally, catamarans move so easily before the wind that a gybe—even in fresh breezes—is no problem at all. One can quite easily catch hold of all the parts of the mainsheet, and heave the sail over by hand, even in quite a large cat. There is seldom anything *like* the pressure in the sail that one experiences in that of a monohull. It is much more like gybing a racing dinghy than a keel-boat—only easier still!

SQUALLS, AND HOW TO COPE WITH THEM

As a general rule, if the headsail is of a size approaching that of the mainsail (bearing in mind the area of a pos-sibly reefed mainsail), then it is the *fore*sheet and not the mainsheet which sould be eased, if the need to let some-thing fly actually occurs. (If full main is set with a much smaller area of headsail, then naturally the mainsheet may be eased first.)

But if the helmsman feels it better to ease her through a violent gust by altering course, let me please stress again that *unless the boat is absolutely hard on the wind, she should be made to bear away* before the squall, and N O T   L U F F E D. That really is most important, and is one of the few things about catamaran handling which is really different from monohull handling. If she is allowed to luff, unless the wind leaves the sails virtually at once, the pressure in them is added to by such considerable centrifugal force that the stability of the craft may be at risk. So, almost always, *bear right away in a squall.*

Sailing close-hauled—as close as she'll comfortably go—when a gust comes, she *can* be luffed, but it *must be done slowly* and smoothly. If the need to spill wind is more urgent than that, let fly (or cut with that sheath-knife) the jibsheets at once.

REACHING TACTICS

Reaching is another matter. Now, if the wind over-does things, there must be no question of luffing—so bear away at once. You are taking the boat along at her fastest—and with the true wind on her beam, she's likely to build up enough speed to draw the apparent wind well ahead. For this reason, when sailing a cat on a reach, it pays to have the sails sheeted in a little tighter than one would in a monohull making good the same course. As speed increases, the wind seems to draw ahead; so she goes faster into it (as it were), which makes it draw further ahead again. If she really gets tramping, one can wind up with the sails almost close-hauled, yet with the true wind broad off.

In order to try and start this process, having laid off a reaching course, it may well pay to bear away a little for a moment just to let her build up speed. Then trim the sheets in as you bring her back on course, and she'll start to fly along.

Even on a broad reach, with the true wind coming in strongly over the quarter, she is quite likely to bring

her apparent wind forward of the beam. It is often worth
deliberately steering off down the face of a sea, to get her
up and sledging. The only danger in doing this is when a
steepish sea comes in from just abaft the beam, because
the lee bow might then, in some boats, try to dig in.
With low freeboard and fine bows, this has to be watched
for, and in these conditions it might be better to bear
away on to a run, or ease her by reefing or by setting
a smaller headsail. Or, of course, dropping the mainsail
altogether.

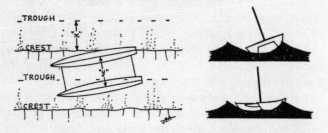

SAILING BEAM ON WHEN "x"="y"
CAN BE UNCOMFORTABLE. A MERE
10° COURSE ALTERATION MAY
MAKE ALL THE DIFFERENCE

In really hard conditions, it will be best to run under
a headsail anyway, and not set any after canvas if possible.
Most cats will make way to windward under a headsail,
so general manoeuvrability will not be greatly impaired.
But when reaching in rough stuff, those cats fitted with
drop-keels should have the lee board lifted right up,
partly to save it from possible damage.

SAIL FULL AND FAST

In a breeze at sea it isn't going to pay well to keep any
catamaran as close to the wind as she'll point, particularly in a big sea. Sail her full and fast, and she'll make
much less leeway and far better up-wind progress all
told. A bit of simple geometry at the chart table will
show what is best. Maybe the choice is five knots and ten
degrees of leeway, or a possible seven knots sailing rather
free, but making only five degrees leeway. That might
well prove best. Do not be dismayed at the sight of deep-
keeled monohulls out-pointing you in a breeze. They
are deep-keeled monohulls; you are in a shoal-draft catamaran. She's a different kind of craft, and is best sailed
in quite a different kind of way.

BIG HEAD SEAS, AND WHAT TO DO WITH THEM

In, say, Force 6 gusting 7, in a single-hulled keel-boat,
when a big crest comes at you and you're close-hauled,
it will probably be best to luff at the last minute, and
take the crest on the bow; then bear away and sail her
full down the back of the wave. You *can* do this in a catamaran, but it will be terribly hard on her if the sea is
really steep, and she is sailing at all fast.

With a catamaran it is generally better to meet the big
seas by bearing *away* as she comes to the top of them,
and then luffing back on course as you go down the back
of it. Just the reverse, in fact, of the usual monohull
method. This way, the catamaran will keep good way on
the whole time; and she will not be given the chance of
'taking off' on the crest.

CATS IN STORMS

I feel sure that most catamaran owners are, like myself, asked again and again how their cats behave in bad weather. This seems to be the thing which worries mono-hull sailors more than anything else—the fact that there is no ballast keel there to hold the boat up in a heavy sea. They tend naturally to think what happens to their monohulls when a sea hits *them* broadside-on and every-thing gets flung over on its beam ends, before the ballast takes charge and brings them violently upright—and swinging over the other way—again. What if you had no ballast—?

My own first-hand knowledge of such conditions is happily fairly limited, but from reading carefully written accounts, and talking to some of those who have endured storms at sea in assorted large and small cruising cata-marans, the general impression seems to be that they actually behave far better than do monohulls.

LIGHTWEIGHT MOTION

The motion, whilst rapid, jerky, and (as one must expect) violent in severe and heavy seas, is nevertheless so damped by a catamaran's broad base and very great initial stability, that on the whole her crew is unlikely to suffer anything like the discomfort that they would experience in a monohull of comparable or even con-siderably greater overall length.

Cooking is unlikely to become impossible, for though the motion is quick, the angles of heel and pitch in-volved are so much smaller than in a ballasted mono-hull, and there is nothing like the momentum and im-petus of the heavier type of vessel to contend with.

Just think of a large sea thrusting up and/or sideways at a single-huller weighing, say, five tons, and imagine the forces involved in accelerating and decelerating that weight so suddenly. And then think of a boat of the same length weighing probably two tons or less on the back of that same sea. Imagine, if you can, what happens when the vessel with the ballast reaches the crest and is literally dropped bodily into the trough—when she arrives at the bottom, she plunges on down ... A *lot* of monohull seamen know the feeling, all too well.

A catamaran, leaping off the crest of the same sea, does not have that impetus, that awful weight lugging her down—she drops the few feet to the trough; checks at once; and goes lifting buoyantly up the next hill, lightly and easily. It is a jolting and unsteady business, to be sure, and hardly enjoyable for anyone, but there is not that ponderous lurching and plunging and rolling which afflicts the crew of a monohull.

BIG BEAM SEAS

A huge and steep beam sea is, of course, the most uncomfortable and, I suppose, the most risky condition for a catamaran to be in. When such conditions arise sufficiently to cause concern (or discomfort) to the crew, in most cases the course may be adjusted so as to close-reach and then broad-reach slightly (the latter being much easier and faster and more comfortable. Sort of 'tacking' *across* the wind, as it were.

When seas are coming in parallel to the hulls, if they are true wind-blown nasties with steep sides and maybe breaking crests, rather than mere swells, a catamaran is of course going to be repeatedly flung to angles approaching the Point of No Return. This angle varies from cat to cat, but most are inherently stable well beyond thirty degrees. On paper, which is very different to flailing along with a press of wind in the sails and a sea shoving up under the weather hull, the danger angle is normally far more than that, as indeed it is likely to be when a cat is lying a-hull with no sail set. But it isn't really a question of angles, so much as of attitude in relation to the water surface. Catamarans retain their natural stability until well after a hull has risen clear of the water. So if you never let a hull lift completely out (and you can sail her *very* hard before that even starts to happen), you are never likely to come anywhere near the capsize point.

In neither of my own cruising cats (nor in anyone else's) have I ever seen the inclinometer read further than twenty-five degrees of heel, and it was only that far round the scale once, by virtue of a sideways jerk at the end of a sudden lurch to leeward when reaching at speed in a confused sea in Force 7. There were still many, many degrees in hand before any risk of coming unstuck even began to accumulate. (We rolled in a further reef, all the same.)

Observation of a model catamaran scaled in size and weights from a rather narrower-than-normal production boat, which was being sailed across the line of 'holiday-beach surf' (representing *enormous* freak seas by scale), showed she had truly amazing ability to keep on her feet. (As of course do full size cats at sea, but it is much easier to describe what occurred with the model, since no one would credit such appalling sea conditions 'for real'.)

When watching the situation in slow motion, what appears to happen is this; the sea approaches the side of the craft, and starts buoying up the weather hull. Now, whereas a ballasted monohull will not begin to heel much at this stage since it takes time to get her weight moving in any new direction, the catamaran will always try to remain at a fairly constant angle to the water surface, so she does start heeling at once.

As the wave advances under her, the cat heels more and and more because the wave-face of course steepens towards its crest. The crest hits her, and she *may* then be flung over a little further. (By now, a monohull has not only been heeled by the sea surface, but by pendulum reaction to the thrust under her weather bilge and also the fact that the surface water is advancing rapidly while her deep keel is held in slower moving water. She is suddenly rolled far over as she reaches the crest, the impact of which is far greater against *her* weight than against the much lighter multihull.)

The crest of a wind-driven sea travels at considerable speed. (Try overtaking one under sail, and you'll know just how fast it's going.) So what one has to bear in mind is just how far it is from the centreline of your catamaran's weather hull to the centreline of her lee hull. Eight feet? Say, three or four metres in a big cat? In any event, it is *not far*. And the wave-crest is advancing quickly from one centreline to the other. The very moment it passes under the middle of the weather hull, that weather hull already begins to drop, and the lee hull —just imagine it in very slow motion—the lee hull is *at once* being lifted and goes on being lifted, until the sea has passed under it. (The 'back' of a wave is never as steep as its face, so there is no risk of being flipped to windward.)

Therefore, it is true to say that even if the weather hull of a beam-on catamaran is flung up so violently as to approach the Point of No Return, the lee hull will practically at once be jerked upwards to provide an opposite 'roll' and restore the balance. The catamaran model was actually flung up like that repeatedly amongst 'huge' foaming crests, but always the crest got under the lee hull just in time to flick her upright again.

SURVIVAL CONDITIONS

But what of very severe conditions, when things are getting a bit much for any kind of sailing? As I have said, running is normally no bother in this type of craft. One may often carry on safely downwind under storm jib, provided there is ample sea-room. When that becomes a doubtful thing to do, the general opinion is that stowing all sail and then towing warps astern is the best answer. It may well be possible to tow one's warps in a long bight, taking one end from each quarter to improve the drag. Like that, there is then little more to do than to keep the cabin door shut, and wait.

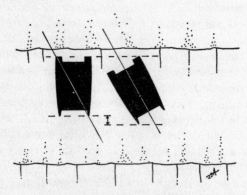

BROAD-REACHING UNDER BARE POLES IN
HEAVY SEAS PROVIDES IN EFFECT A
LONGER W.L. LENGTH THAN WHEN
RUNNING

Some ocean-going cat skippers have maintained that it is better to stream warps from one quarter only, and steer by hand if need be; and there is good reasoning behind this. A catamaran whose overall length is, for instance, thirty feet, and which has a normal beam of between fourteen and fifteen feet, will have a *diagonal* length, from one bow to the opposite stern, of something in the order of not thirty, but thirty-three feet. Thinking in terms of running before an ocean storm in which one might be overtaken by a 'rogue' sea, obviously a thirty-three-foot boat is better off than one three feet shorter. Hence the theory that it is better not to run a cat off dead before storms, but rather to take the seas slightly on one quarter.

Bernard Moitessier, that extraordinary French man-of-the-sea who sailed his steel monohull ketch *Joshua* non-stop once-and-a-half round the world, has long maintained that, even in his type of yacht, it is safer to run in ocean storms with the seas on the quarter (just), rather than absolutely dead astern. In this way the rudder remains efficient because there is water pressure constantly on one side of it, and you can, he says, therefore always steer clear of the bad crests, or at least keep control far better than if running dead before, with a comparatively 'dead' rudder.

Naturally there will be times when one does not have sea-room enough to go running downwind. Then the alternatives are heaving-to (while that is possible), or lying a-hull more or less beam-on to the seas.

HEAVING-TO

Some cats heave-to very well indeed, lying as steady as a duck, and laughing at the elements; in which case, happy are their crews. But most cats, being exceptionally shal-low-drafted things, do tend to 'hunt'—wavering around all over the place, surging forward, swinging up almost head-to, then making a sternboard, bearing away and swooping forward again.

Boats which behave this way hove-to can be tamed to some extent by not sheeting either of the balancing sails (i.e. main and jib) at all flat. If the headsail is eased so that it curves well in towards the mast before being held to weather by sheet-lead or shroud position, it will be a more effective 'brake' than if flat and taut. It may be necessary to ease the mainsheet (in our Catalac for ex-ample, until the boom-end is over the lee corner of the cockpit), so that it will not drive her round close to the wind. The helm may then be adjusted to keep her steady, or as steady as possible, perhaps by putting it slightly a-lee. In that attitude, she should fore-reach at a knot or two, and with luck will just about hold her own, in the sense of not loosing ground to leeward.

LYING A-HULL

Having reached the point when progress under sail (even hove-to) is no longer possible, lying a-hull under bare rigging may be all that's left, and most catamarans for-tunately do this well and very safely. It is best if they can be trimmed by rudder or by warps etc., to lie not *exactly* parallel to the seas. Most boats will lie naturally at a slight angle anyway.

The important thing when lying a-hull in heavy weather in a cat fitted with drop-keels, is to lift the lee one completely, and the weather one too unless the pre-vention of sideways drift is considered absolutely vital. The more easily the boat can be pushed sideways by the crests, the safer she will be—and the more comfortable.

But let's get away from all that broken water and find a sheltered anchorage instead. Catamarans have both advantages and disadvantages, when it comes to anchoring.

ANCHORING PROCEDURES

To be gloomy, let's look at the drawbacks first. Mostly, catamarans are very light boats, and should be kept as light as is reasonably possible; so the use of all-chain anchor cable is not necessarily the best idea—particularly if the chain is stowed right up forward. One could of course have an anchor winch on the cabintop by the mast and stow the cable amidships on a lower part of the bridgedeck, but so far no production catamarans are to my knowledge fitted this way.

In the medium and smaller range of cats, an anchor winch on the foredeck is not really ideal, since there is not normally enough height in the chain-locker on the bridgedeck at that point to let the chain or warp stow itself as it comes off the gypsy. A winch on cabintop or mast would give the necessary elevation, though again, such a fitting would in itself have to be of the lightest possible material and construction consistent with adequate strength. Weight high up is always to be avoided if possible, though here some compensation would be derived because any chain cable is likely to come to rest lower down in the bridgedeck than if under the foredeck.

LYING TO ROPE CABLE

Most catamarans anchor to three or four fathoms of chain (that's around six or seven metres), and the rest is then rope—with the usual drawback that one needs to put out greater scope when lying to rope than one does with chain alone.

A CQR anchor needs, they say, a chain four times the depth of the water. That being so, five, or in strong winds six times the depth may be required when lying to rope. Which is all very well when there is nobody anchored just astern of you, and you have lots and lots of swinging room, especially at low tide. Not only will you take up more space than your chain-rode neighbours, but with every flukey wind-shift, be it a squall or even a faint air, a catamaran will pull her rope at once over the bottom to swing into line with the new direction (her light draft doing little to prevent her), whereas chain-rode monohulls tend to 'stay put' for quite a time longer.

ANCHOR WEIGHTS

Fortunately there is at least a partial way out of this problem. I have for years now, used an anchor weight which, when lowered down the cable until just clear of the bottom, makes the anchor rope behave much more like chain, reducing one's swing, and also allowing us safely to reduce the scope—a boon in really crowded anchorages. The one we have is a singularly handy and satisfactory thing specially designed for the job, called a 'Chum' (manufactured by Frank Gibson Ltd., 543 Gorgie Road, Edinburgh). It consists of a specially shaped large shackle with a handle which, when lifted, automatically opens the shackle, so that one can easily drop it over or lift it off the anchor cable. It can then be slid down into the depths on a suitable line. From the shackle hangs a weight on the end of a stalk, and the stalk is designed so that a number of specially-shaped lead 'biscuits' can be added, to build the total weight up as required by the size and windage of one's particular boat.

The basic shackle-and-weight weighs 23 lb (10.4 kilos), each additional biscuit adding a further 14 lb (6.4 kilos). In our nine-metre cat we use the weight and one biscuit, but she has a lot of freeboard forward, and in one squall I have seen that lifted to the surface, so perhaps a second biscuit might be useful in preventing snubbing—not that snubbing is a real problem when lying to nylon anchor warp. (It should be nylon, rather than a less stretchable fibre.) Any kind of weight slid down on a big shackle would do the job just as well, of course, but this 'Chum' thing has the advantage of being easily fitted and removed with one hand, and you do not have to hump the whole thing at once if you don't want to. The biscuits can be lifted straight off and carried separately, and people with 'discs', or 'hearts', will know the value of that!

As to the winch difficulty, one blessing of the chain-cum-warp arrangement is that even when anchoring in deep water it is normally very much lighter to pull in than an all-chain cable, so the actual need for a winch is less. Rope comes in easily once you have got her moving towards the anchor (a touch ahead with the engine would help, of course), and it may be possible to coil the warp down into its locker as it comes in. If you are careful to let it lie naturally there, a soft-laid rope being better than a very stiff one, it should never snare or snag when you are letting go.

If the catamaran tends to sheer about at anchor, and some of them do, there are two things which can be tried to hold her more steadily. The simple answer is instead of lying to a centrally placed fairlead, moor her by one or other bow. This will give her a natural sheer (belay on the port bow and she'll sheer to starboard, etc.) which should steady her up considerably. Alternatively, one can rig a span (or 'bridle' if you prefer it).

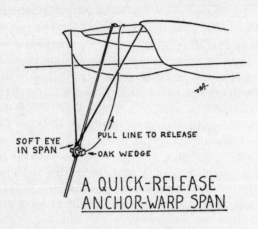

SOFT EYE IN SPAN

PULL LINE TO RELEASE

OAK WEDGE

A QUICK-RELEASE ANCHOR-WARP SPAN

SPANS AND BRIDLES

In *Aku-Aku* we devised a span (bridle) which consists of a softly laid-up braided rope, around the same length as our waterline (about 25 ft.). It has a loop at each end which drops over a bollard on the end of each bow. At its middle is another loop, and through this a bight of the centrally hung anchor warp is poked, and a short and narrow oak wedge is driven through to hold the bight in place. This is done on deck, between the main bollard and the cable-roller, after the hook is down and the scope adjusted. The end of a light line from the wide end of the wedge is made fast on deck, and is of such a length as to remain slack when the anchor cable is eventually veered until the two arms of the span, from the bow ends, are sharing the weight with the cable. The cable is of course trapped in the central loop by the wedge.

It has always worked very well, and is quick and simple to rig. But more important still is that it can be released instantly if you have, for instance, to veer more cable in a hurry, or weigh anchor. A sharp tug on the light line at once jerks the oak wedge out of the loop, and the anchor cable is immediately freed. The span can be retrieved in due course, and so long as it and the wedge line are secured and not of such a length as to reach the propeller, one can even motor away while sorting it out at leisure. But in use it does stop her sheering about very successfully.

CABLE AND ANCHOR STOWAGE

In most production cats, a cable locker is sited more or less centrally on the foredeck, the one big advantage being that it can be completely self-draining through holes in the bridgedeck. One can therefore stow the cable as it comes in, and chuck a few bucketfuls of sea in after it to clean and sweeten it up when you're done.

In the Catalac and also in our Prout Ranger, we used a 35-lb CQR bower anchor (a 25-lb one would do, but I am fond of that particular anchor, and trust it). In each boat (as in most GRP cats) the bridgedeck cable locker has had a hatch which enabled us to stow anchor and all inside, so as to leave a clear and uncluttered deck. For an anchor of this size one needs a hatch opening only just over a foot (0.30 metres) square. As it happens, the Catalac's deck also has a moulded stowage place for a 25-lb Meon (Danforth) type anchor, which is very neat and convenient too, but I happen to prefer the

CQR for use in the kelp and stones of the West Coast of Scotland, where our boat is based.

SHOAL-DRAFT ANCHORAGES

The greatest advantage of all when anchoring a catamaran however, lies in the fact that being mostly of very shallow draft, and able to take the ground happily in suitable places, one can usually anchor in shallower water than most other cruising boats—so one seldom needs to put out—or haul in—much scope of cable anyway. This all means that Father will probably be quite willing to drop the hook two, or even three or four times in the course of a day's pottering, to let the family explore new creeks, beaches or bays. But because even catamarans with stub keels may sink into mud on taking the ground, fisherman-type anchors are best avoided! With tidal currents and a cross wind, you never know where she might sit down...

To my way of thinking, this shallow water anchoring business is one of the greatest joys of cruising in a catamaran—it has certainly given our family many very happy hours of fun, and has allowed us to explore countless places we would (and did) sail by, time and again, in a monohull of the same size.

10

Engines and
Handling Under Power

There is little point in elaborating on the statement that
catamarans (like any boats) are going to handle differently
depending on their own individual hull shapes, and the
type, variety or number of engines fitted. So much is
obvious. So first let's have a glance at what kinds of
mechanical power can be installed.

Provided it is not heavy, any kind of motor may be
fitted into most of the large and medium-sized catamarans, but the smaller ones such as the now out-of-
production Ranger 27s and 31s, Iroquois Mk I, Bobcat,
and the Hirondelle, and most of the Wharram designs,
are usually fitted with outboard motors, simply because
there is no room to fit an inboard one.

ENGINE SIZE

There are many advantages in the outboard motor, anyway—the only real snag being that they are fearfully
inefficient by comparison to inboards. This means that
whereas an 8hp diesel or a 12hp petrol inboard would
suffice as an auxiliary, the equivalent power in actual
performance will barely be produced by a 20hp outboard.
Indeed, for catamarans over about 28 feet (8.5 metres),

191

something around 33 to 40hp is going to be most satisfactory.

While a pretty minute outboard will push an easily
driven thing like a catamaran in a calm (I have seen a
1¼ hp Seagull give a 27-foot cat over 2 knots), if there is
any headwind at all, it is going to be very hard on fuel
to be mean with the horsepower, and the usual petrol/
oil mixture is expensive. It seems to work out cheaper
in the long run to buy a bigger engine and run it at
half throttle or so for cruising purposes.

Our little *Twintail*, for example, started life with a
9½hp outboard, which in a calm gave her just short of five
knots flat out, even when the correct propeller for the
job was eventually fitted. Four-and-a-half knots was a
good deal more economical with that engine, but that
still left us burning something approaching 1½ gallons
an hour. Eventually we fitted her with a 20hp motor of
the same make, which gave the far better figures of a
top speed at six-and-a-half knots, cruising speed five
knots, and consumption *reduced* to 1¼ gallons an hour.

Aku-Aku, on the other hand, has a similar waterline
length when under way, and she sports a 33hp outboard
from the same maker. This gives her a flat-out run at a
little over 6¾ knots, and cruising at 5¼ she burns up only
just over a gallon an hour, if that. Which rather suggests
that it is cheaper to slightly over-power the boat than
to have a small engine struggling for breath.

In a sailing catamaran, however, there is very little
point in trying to burst the 'eight-knot barrier' by motor
alone. Of course it *can* be done, but the large engines
which would be needed and the weight of them (not to
mention any propeller drag) would have an *awful* effect
on her sailing performance.

OUTBOARDS AND CAVITATION

The chief disadvantage of outboard motors, apart from the cost of feeding them, is that unless they can be positioned well forward in a catamaran, for instance somewhere under the *forward* end of the cockpit, they do tend to encounter severe cavitation problems in anything of a lop, or if heavy crew members go to help each other on the foredeck.

Mostly, outboards tend to be hung at the after end of the cockpit or over the cockpit transom, so crew weight moving on to the bows may have a particularly bad effect in the smaller cat. Such engines are, however, usually hung on a bracket which may be to some extent retractable. But even so, one is faced with the need for not just Long-Shaft versions, but usually Extra-Long-Shaft extensions, because with no boat in the water just above the propeller there is nothing other than the motor's own tiny 'cavitation plate' to prevent air being sucked down to the prop.

Even worse is the fact that most outboards are hung very near the extreme stern of the boat, so that any pitching raises and lowers the prop by a considerable amount. At certain speeds also, the boat's own quarter waves may do nothing at all to help. But the real problem lies in the fact that at any speed much over four knots or so, the propeller mounted between the hulls will always suffer from trying to work in highly aerated water thrown into its path by the two meeting bow-waves.

The only part-solution, is to get the propeller down as deep as possible—which means a very strong bracket, and usually some method of protecting the motor itself from the spray and seas which slop about down there

Then comes the added difficulty of tilting the motor clear of the water when sailing—for if possible it should be clear enough that a sea bursting across the sterns in a gale or something (tide race, maybe) will not twist the poor thing off its clamps, or wreck the bracket. But there is no doubt that it is worth being able to get it clear of the water, if only to save the quarter or even half knot of drag which a propeller will otherwise apply when sailing.

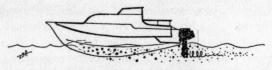

AERATED FLOW FROM INNER BOW-WAVES
ENCOURAGES CAVITATION

Being able to reduce the drag like that is one of the big advantages of an outboard—another is that for servicing it can be fairly readily taken ashore or hoisted into the cockpit, maybe using the boom and mainsheet as a derrick. But there is a further advantage. So long as the outboard can be readily connected to the ship's steering linkage when in use, with remote controls by the wheel the boat will prove highly manoeuvrable, and, to use what is now a thoroughly old-fashioned saying, can be made to 'turn on a sixpence' with the greatest of ease.

MANOEUVRING UNDER POWER

When handling any catamaran under power, it must be remembered that one is dealing with a shallow craft which carries considerable windage in comparison to her grip on the water. For this reason, manoeuvring in confined waters in a stiff breeze may not be completely straightforward, for as soon as the speed drops, the boat may well tend to blow off downwind. Cats fitted with drop-keels should if possible leave these at least half down while motoring—those designed without such protuberances will have short keels or hulls which naturally have greater grip on the water anyway—but even then the shoal-draft effect must be borne in mind.

There are one or two catamarans which manage on a single inboard engine. One of these, the Heavenly Twins centre-cockpit sloop, has made use of a hydraulic drive unit, the Nash HyDrive, mounted on a hinged 'leg'. This is placed well in under the middle of the boat to reduce cavitation through pitching, and her central 'pod' lets her make use of a diesel engine low in the cockpit where the smells cannot get into the accommodation. Prout's Snowgoose 34 has a similar set-up in the pod, or 'nacelle' as they call it, rather nearer the stern of the boat and using a long extension 'out-drive' unit. Both craft can of course be fitted with an outboard instead.

Other single-engined catamarans, some 30-foot Oceanics for example, and one or two Bobcats (neither of which is still being built) have simply installed a normal marine inboard with conventional stern-tube, shaft and propeller in one hull only. So long as the helmsman appreciates that she will then turn much tighter on one lock than on the other, and that in a crosswind things may require a bit of forethought, this is of course perfectly all right, at least when under way at sea. As far as I can gather, even those catamarans fitted with a pair of inboards, one in each hull, are quite often seen to be using only one of them when at sea.

TWIN-ENGINED VERSATILITY

A pair of engines, mounted one in each stern and either with out-drives which I would think in small boats anyway, must have some cavitational problems in a seaway, or with conventional stern-tubes and under-the-hull propellers (which would be largely cavitation-free), will naturally provide one with phenomenal manoeuvring capabilities, since they are spaced so widely apart. A touch ahead on one and astern on the other, and the boat will twiddle round so smartly as to have the foredeck hands staggering backwards across the deck! If these engines are diesels, one has economy, speed, manoeuvrability—and more vibration than with petrol engines, especially in GRP cats; the trouble there being that, unlike in a monohull, there is no vast chunk of metal to absorb the shudders. Even so ...

ONE ENGINE, TWO PROPS?

One or two boats are now trying a single engine coupled with hydraulic drives to twin propellers, one under each hull. Although there is some loss of efficiency with this kind of drive, the latest versions are not all that far behind mechanical couplings, and in fact do have many advantages, in that the motor itself can be installed just about wherever you fancy in the boat. The control valves enable you to run the flow separately to either propeller, forward or reverse; or to both props at once, both forward or both astern. Such an installation works out cheaper than a full twin-engined system, and has most of the advantages, though not all.

In the motor-sailer category of cat, where sailing performance is not the main object, I think I would be happier (supposing my pocket to be the right size) to have two entirely separate engine systems, with normal 3-bladed propellers and through-the-hull sterngear. The drag when sailing would of course mean the loss of up to $\frac{3}{4}$ of a knot or so, and goodness knows what would happen when you sailed over a dense patch of seaweed, but this would be without doubt the best arrangement when actually motoring, both at sea and in port.

POWER CATS

It really is the strangest thing. There are very, very few proper power catamarans. And no one, so far, has been able to explain to me *why* this should be.

When you think of it, the one drawback which is suffered worst of all by any conventional motor yacht, however large or small she may be, is that with the sea on the quarter, the beam, or the bow (in fact, anywhere other than dead ahead), they roll, and roll wickedly. Some less than others, of course. Those whose size and owner's wealth is big enough to run to stabilisers are better off—though personally I have never liked the particular brand of motion which stabilizers produce.

The *only* time a catamaran 'rolls', is when a steep sea comes at her exactly beam on. Luff or bear away a few degrees, and all is smooth—the family or guests can relax in a remarkably steady environment, and there is no need for expensive machinery to keep things that way.

Ideally, of course, a pure powerboat should be designed as such, but in many respects, some sailing catamaran hulls are, both above and below water, not unlike those of drawn-out powerboats. Everyone knows the success that catamaran-type racing speedboats have been enjoying.

197

So why is there hardly any demand—so far—for cata-maran motor cruisers? For a great number of years now powered catamarans have been in constant use in many parts of the world as workboats and survey craft. The Prouts of Canvey Island have long been producing such craft, based on their normal, sailing-cruiser hulls. One would think that this was advertisement enough, but apparently it isn't. Many Bill O'Brien designs would make quite passable motor yachts; so too would be the Catalac, but there it is ... The world of marine motorists seems to have decided that 'catamarans are sailing boats', and therefore are only suitable as such!

I know this much; if ever Judy and I are too old and decrepit to handle sails, we shall sell our mast and rig and convert our current catamaran completely to power. Motor in each hull, with separate electrics, fuel and all. I'll have a permanently covered steering position, and a power anchor winch and self-stowing hook, and shall only visit the foredeck to sunbathe—with a rug and deck-chair, of course.

11

Accommodation Above
and Below Decks

Although it is probably true to say that when people are choosing a boat, one of the very first things they consider is the accommodation offered, I have deliberately left discussion of that to near the end of this book. Here again, it is largely a matter of personal preference. Some people feel they are never going to need a boat with five berths, whereas for others the thought of being able to sleep eight or ten comfortably is enough to make them start feeling for their cheque-books.

And one does not have to have a very big catamaran in order to have bunks for eight; most thirty-footers (nine- to ten-metre boats) sleep around five or six in permanently made-up bunks, and the saloon area will likely accommodate two more, possibly without even having to do things with the cabin table. And apart from the Wharram type with its lack of bridgedeck accommodation and its very fine 'V' hulls, even the smallest cruising catamarans can sleep up to five, and usually have three permanent bunks anyway.

Along with shoal-draft benefits and steadiness at sea, one of the chief advantages of catamarans for cruising is that their general shape lends itself to a type of accommodation layout which provides lots of space, yet with a fair amount of privacy. Your bunk is your own, and doesn't necessarily have to become a seat, or part of the dinner table, or be lifted up to let folk use the loo (as in so many tris and monohulls). It remains somewhere that you can rest your weary bones, or laze at length with a book, without having to inconvenience others. You can sleep in peace, when having a spot of off-watch shut-eye during the day, knowing that it is your space, and no one is likely to come rooting under your feet for the next chart or can of beans. Better than that; you know you are not going to be suddenly tipped on to the floor-boards just because some clot on deck gybes unexpectedly, or tacks the ship in a breeze. You may very likely (even in a small cruising cat) have a proper little cabin, all to yourself—or one with a grand big double-bunk ...

THE BEST PLACE FOR BUNKS

In cats under about ten metres long, when sailing in brisk breezes, the prudent skipper should beware, as I have already said, the effects of letting anyone spend long periods up in the lee bow—whether on deck or below. In-the-hull bunks placed right forward may there-fore not be the best idea for use under way in certain conditions.

Because of this, it is better, unless the cat herself is over thirty feet in length, to look for a design in which all the forward bunks are situated on the bridgedeck rather than down in the bows. Then dormant souls keep their weight nearer the craft's centreline where they won't add at all to the boat's heeling angle.

Further aft, bunks may be put anywhere to advantage, though under way occupants will have a quieter time of it on the bridgedeck than in passage berths or 'tunnel cabins' under the cockpit seats. And the best place of all

must surely be on the bridgedeck, right aft in a stern
cabin. So far, at the time of writing, only one small production catamaran, P.T. Yachts' Heavenly Twins 26-
footer, has been designed with proper stern cabins. Her
excellent layout comprises a pair of separate double-berth
cabins abaft the central cockpit, and what amounts to a
'day cabin' forward with two settee-berths in the saloon,
large galley, separate chart-space and a washroom. *All*
six bunks are thus on the bridgedeck. Designed purely
for sea-going cruising with halyards, sheets, and all
engine controls in the cockpit (including that which lifts
the big propeller clear of the 'oggin when one is sailing),
she displays all the results of the very considerable sea-
and-ocean-going experience of her designer.

'HEADS'—OR TAILS

Because of the business of weight right forward in a hull,
I am not terribly happy about smaller cats which have
the heads compartment up in one bow (see page 118).
Crew weight, shut in there and maybe not in a position
to move aft without due notice, should this become advisable, can at times be awkward. I recall one crossing
of the North Channel at the start of a cruise to Scottish
waters in our first cat. My crew that day was unfortunately
suffering from some kind of tummy upset, and the loo
was right up forward in what just happened then to be
the lee bow. There was quite a sea running, and under a
particularly gloomy cloud the wind suddenly increased.
No shouts of mine could be heard down there behind
the closed door, for at that speed there was a lot of water
noise forward. I couldn't leave the wheel, because under
what was suddenly a press of sail, the lee bow was sub-
merging to deck level, and apart from the obvious danger

of it eventually tripping her up, it kept making her try to luff round against the helm. I was able to bear away, but had then to continue running downwind until my poor crew was able to come aft. It wasn't much of a joke at the time, nor was it really a terribly dangerous moment—but *could* have been so.

THE GALLEY GLORIOUS

Galleys, since they do not suffer the motion and heeling of a monohull, can be sited almost anywhere in a cat,

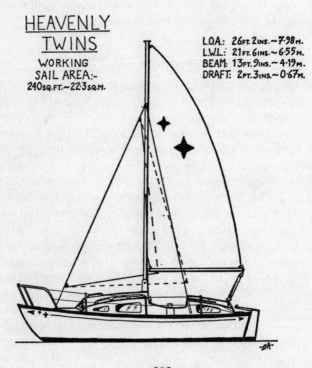

HEAVENLY
TWINS
WORKING
SAIL AREA:-
240 SQ.FT. ~ 22·3 SQ.M.

L.O.A.: 26 FT. 2 INS. ~ 7·98 M.
L.W.L.: 21 FT. 6 INS. ~ 6·55 M.
BEAM: 13 FT. 9 INS. ~ 4·19 M.
DRAFT: 2 FT. 3 INS. ~ 0·67 M.

though again preferably not too far forward, this time because of all the stores which one likes to have to hand when cooking. The usual thing is to take up the central portion of one hull (traditionally the port hull in any small sailing vessel, originally because when one hove-to to cook and prepare food, one did so on the starboard tack so that other vessels would give way to you, and the galley was then where things wouldn't fall out of it or spill hot things over your legs).

In a catamaran it may all be beautifully laid out in a long line of cooker, draining board, sink, working-top

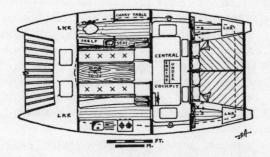

HEAVENLY TWINS. Designed by P. M. Patterson; sold by Aquarius Marine, Gweek Quay, Gweek, Helston, Cornwall. GRP construction. Low aspect-ratio keels, skegs, and fixed-draft rudders. Wheel steering in cosy central cockpit. Mast and all halyards convenient to helmsman. Diesel (or outboard) mounted in central pod (nacelle) in cockpit. Pod also provides good saloon headroom. Accommodation for 6 in two double-berth stern-cabins and saloon. Every inch a cruising boat, and no pretentions at racing performance, yet capable of good average speeds. Very strongly built, and a grand little seaboat. Handles with delightful ease.

and so on, and there will usually be room for a small fridge or ice-box, as well as for masses of stowage. Never before in the history of small boat sailing have such magnificent or easily-worked galleys been possible. This is just one of the many features which make catamarans so utterly ideal for family sailing.

SPACE HEATING PROBLEMS

While on the subject of cooking, heating the crew in a catamaran may not be quite so straightforward. Perhaps the chap with a much-used inboard engine, or who doesn't mind running a generator in a cat big enough to carry the weight of forced-draught central heating, will find no difficulty. Those of us with less than that do have some problems, though. In most production cats at any rate it is not easy to find space for a built-in cabin stove in the saloon area. And while it may be possible to toast yourself at that level by some means or other, the heat from there is unlikely to permeate downwards into the hulls.

One well-tried answer is to have a couple (preferably) of catalytic heaters, or something of the sort, which can be placed so as to warm each hull—the heat will naturally rise up into the bridgedeck area and warm that as well. Even though this may not be as nice as the cosy glow of a bogey stove burning driftwood or whatever, it is thus reasonably easy to keep the temperature up to a pleasant degree even in winter.

In our own boat, we find that a meths-burning thing called the Origo Heat-Pal gives us satisfactory warmth at least for those end-of-season evenings, and being unspillable it is pretty safe, too. After dark we often supplement it with a pair of large-wick paraffin table-lamps, which give a cosier, less harsh (and cheaper) light than the ship's electrics. (With the fabric-covered deckhead not far above the glass 'chimneys', one has however to be careful how one places these, and we do not use them at sea. Normally, at anchor, they help generate a very snug fug indeed. But ...)

VENTILATION

The big danger with any stove in a small boat is that of ventilation. No matter how cold it is outside, adequate ventilation must be kept open when burning anything. And heaters should not be left burning at night, or the oxygen consumption may prove fatal with surprising speed to anyone sleeping low down in a hull. I am sad to say that I know of at least three catamarans in which this has happened tragically.

Ventilation in cats is not much of a problem, since few of them, sailing always upright, tend to throw water about the way a monohull does. Opening windows *à la* motor yacht can therefore be used in addition to the usual deck vents. However, if I were to use a catamaran fitted with opening windows, or indeed the very large fixed windows which coastal craft can safely enjoy, for ocean sailing, I think it would be best to provide storm shutters of some kind. Although catamarans don't normally take solid water on deck the way a single-hulled yacht can, in very severe conditions it is naturally to be expected sooner or later that a sea will 'catch her wrong'.

COCKPIT AND DRAINS

The very big cockpits which most production cats proudly sport—and which are one of their many delights when the sun shines—are often regarded with deep suspicion by monohull sailors, who are used to the possibility of shipping the odd sea aft. However, after years of cruising in cats, sometimes in surprisingly steep seas, I have personally never seen more than light spray reach the cockpit. Even so, large cockpit drains are easy enough to arrange in this kind of boat, since the outlets are more than likely to be above waterlevel. Yet in my opinion, they are seldom big enough to cope with a real emergency in most production boats.

In almost the same breath, I must mention that I know of a certain Prout Ranger 27 whose big cockpit filled completely when she was sailed through a severe tide race in bad weather. 'Seas fell vertically into it', as the owner put it. It never had time to drain through its small outlets, but it seems the motion spilled quite a bit out over the stern. The cabin doors were of course closed, though I imagine some water found its way below. But such is the natural buoyancy of a catamaran, that she slowly sailed on and out into smoother water, and the cockpit eventually emptied in the normal way.

Really large cockpits of the kind which monohull sailors fear so much create little danger in catamarans. They are basically 'dry' boats, and as most catamariners know, the wearing of oilskins depends only on whether or not it is *raining*, in all but quite strong wind and sea situations.

HELMSMAN PROTECTION, WHEEL AND TILLER STEERING

For sailing in northern waters (and I include all British waters in that group), I feel that the helmsman at least should be given as much protection from wind and weather as possible. From this point of view, wheel steering is an improvement on tiller steering, in that the wheel may often be positioned on the after cabin bulkhead, so that one can sit or stand in its lee when beating to windward on a wet summer's day.

Some boats, like Sailcraft's big Cherokee, and the nine-metre Catalac, have been thoughtfully designed with a special little helmsman's nook at the forward end of the cockpit, which can then be covered right over with either a spray hood, or a permanent 'hard-top'. My own preference is for a hood which can be folded down to let one fully enjoy the sun and fresh air when they are around, and which will afford surprising warmth and dryness on the wettest of night passages when rigged. This particular sort of cockpit layout has other advantages, in that the doorway to the accommodation is in the same nook, and the little dry area of the deck at the 'doorstep', so to speak, means a lot less water is carried below on sailing boots. That a helmsman's chair adds to the general luxury, without being in the way when sheet handling, need hardly be said.

Many catamarans, because of high superstructure forward of the cockpit, do not provide seating for the man at the wheel, and I feel this is a pity, since, for instance, an awful lot of Dads have to spend much of their time at sea there, while Mum tends to the kiddies at the cabin table. It can be very hard on the feet after about ten hours...

SNAGS WITH TILLERS

There is just this to be said for tiller steering (with or without some kind of tiller extensions); one can at least sit down on the side-benches in the cockpit. It is my good fortune to have done 'trial sails' in most British makes of catamaran, and not one of them have I found quite so nice to *tiller*-steer as the majority of monohulls, when in a seaway. This has nothing to do with the amount of effort involved, for the majority of well-designed cats either have balanced rudders or are well-balanced boats in the first place.

Tiller-steered cats are fine in still water, but as soon as anything of a lop gets up, one may experience an unpredictable small jerking of the tiller (never all that violent admittedly, but there all the same), which is occasioned by waves affecting first the one rudder and then the other. They hardly ever seem to be under exactly the same side-pressures at the same moment, and this transmits via the tiller crossbar an uneven movement to the helmsman's wrist which although it may not amount to much, becomes tiring after a long period.

Wheel steering, with its necessary friction as the lines pass round their leads, is able to absorb this. If the leverages are correctly worked out, the normal 'feel' of a sailing boat can still be there under one's hand, but the unpleasant vibrations and shudders have gone, leaving the boat a joy to steer. Still, some people say they can't bear wheel steering.

AUTOMATIC HELMSMEN

Some people say they can't bear to sit and steer anyway, and prefer a boat which can be made to steer herself. As it happens, many catamarans do have exceptionally good directional stability, and with sheets carefully trimmed and helm adjusted and 'locked', they can often be made to sail themselves well enough to let one have a quick check on the charts anyway. Some will hold a course to windward or even downwind for hours, without attention.

In *Aku-Aku* we have a hinged plywood flap on the cabin bulkhead behind the wheel. This is of such a shape that when pushed down, its plastic-lined edge jams firmly against the wheel's rim, allowing the helm to be locked in any position. To release it suddenly, one simply gives the wheel a good jerk, folding the flap out of the way afterwards. In *Twintail* we had a line and quick-release clamp on the tiller crossbar, which worked every bit as well. In her we also had a most effective wind-vane, which Michael Henderson designed for us, and which proved so successful that similar copies have been fitted to many Prout catamarans.

Wind-vanes and catamarans are an interesting mixture. In one sense it is a nearly perfect combination, because cats have this tendency to sail straight anyway. With balanced main rudders, the wind-vane can be connected direct to the boat's normal steering gear, doing away with any need for servo blades or other gadgetry. However, if vanes are used where wind strength, as well as direction, is continually altering, frequent adjusting may be necessary even with the best gear. Cats are particularly sensitive to such fluctuations, because an increase of any kind in the wind-speed will make them accelerate noticeably. This at once makes the apparent wind draw ahead, and as your vane is worked by the apparent wind direction, the cat will more than probably cease to remain on course.

I feel that catamarans might thus be better off with a mechanical 'auto-pilot' working off a magnetic compass and ignoring the wind altogether, but such things do consume electricity, which means charging the batteries more frequently.

The one redeeming feature in this whole business, is that as *catamarans are anyway very much less exhausting to steer* than are monohulls, automatic steering devices are therefore more of a luxury than a necessity, even for the single-hander.

AIDS TO NAVIGATION

This really applies to any boat, and not just catamarans, but in a cat, with her spacious cockpit, one has a better chance of achieving all sorts of ideals. It is a great help if there is somewhere convenient to the helmsman for placing the like of pilot books and a detail chart (be it in one of those plastic covers). These items are not going to be needed there at sea, of course, for with luck the boat will have a decent chart-table somewhere below for real navigation. But for pilotage close in-shore, in and out of creeks and harbours, up lochs and rivermouths, or for rock-dodging along the French coast maybe, life is much easier for the man at the wheel if he can see at a glance where he is and what to look out for next. An echo-sounder *readable from the helm* is likewise far more use than one tucked away by the chart-space down below.

In our own boat, we use a Woolworth's plastic kitchen trough to hold binoculars, cameras and deck-log by the helm (but well away from the compass), while a chart-case can be held by shock-cords on the open cabin door alongside the steering position. It can't blow away, and when the door is closed in the evening, we can sit round the cabin table and look at the chart to see where it was we went wrong, and maybe discuss what we'll do instead, tomorrow...

CREWS IN CONTACT

In any event, in catamarans, one usually has this 'togetherness' of on-watch crew and off-watch crew. The helmsman is almost always on about the same level as those seated in the saloon, so, as I said earlier, the family need not ever feel 'cut off' in any way. They can in all probability see out of the eye-level windows in nearly all directions, with the result that even when the going gets rough and both Dad *and* Mum are doing wild exercises on deck and the sails are rattling and it might otherwise seem somewhat frightening, the kids below can feel themselves part of what is going on and not out of touch in any way.

Wharram catamarans are the exception to this, in that their slatted bridgedecks are devoid of deck-houses, and the hulls are thus very much two separate boats, into which one climbs down a series of steps. Once in there, all is very snug indeed, and divorced from the conditions on deck, and the knowledge that the seas can do their worst and burst all over her without causing trouble must be worth a lot—provided things are properly constructed, properly secured, and snugged down, and that one has plenty of sea-room, that is!

TRAMPOLINES AND SLATS

Both a number of production designs and Wharram's 'Polynesian' cats have them, but I personally dislike the use of netting or webbing 'trampolines' to fill the undecked spaces between bows and/or sterns. To my way of thinking, firm, solid footing is essential on any foredeck (if only to avoid having the motion accentuated by a flexible substance), and where such space-fillers between the hulls are required I prefer something like the timber slatting used in Heavenly Twins, rather than floppy string or fabric contraptions. But I'll grant you that when you do fall over on the latter, you are going to have a softer landing!

HAND-GRIPS AND HARNESSES

Something firm to grip is important everywhere, on any sailing vessel. Many folk seem to think that since cats do not heel nor roll, and mostly sail steadily upright, there is little need for things to hold on to. Certainly catamarans will rarely try to slide your feet from under you, but the motion can be very jerky indeed at speed, and can be most unpredictable in direction at that! So it seems to me that in every possible place where some kind of rail or post or grip is likely to be required, whether above or below decks, between ready-made items like shrouds for instance, a catamaran should so be fitted.

I know that many catamariners (particularly those whose boats are built with very narrow side-decks) claim that guard-rails round the ship are unnecessary, and all you need is a decent pulpit forward. From my own experience, in most production cats which can be fitted with proper guard-rails, I have always been glad to have that extra security, especially if children are going to sail in them.

A catamaran's decks usually *are* nice and steady, but the difficulty comes when leaving or entering the cockpit, and also at the foredeck-end of the cabintop. Say one has just changed jibs or something—there is one heck of a gap between the forestay and the corner of the cabintop-handrail in most cats, and the sea awaits if she lurches and you overshoot! With a guard-rail, be it of the usual plastic coated wire, or my own preference of pre-stretched Terylene rope led through the staunchions, at least one has something with which to check one's flight.

Wharram's catamarans are (again) the one exception, of course. In them you seldom have any reason to go anywhere near the sides of the ship. Everything happens in the middle, between the cabintops. Those very separated hulls in his boats have, by the way, another advantage, suppose you are having an 'off day', and the others want an uproarious party. You can always find total peace by shutting yourself into the other hull! It's just a pity that in order to sleep a reasonable number of folk in uncramped bunks, you need a *very large* Wharram cat. She will be cheap enough to build, of course. Even professionally built, they work out cheaper than anything else that size—though I think one should bear in mind possible berthing dues later on! You would not, however, be the first to build a Wharram boat and sail off to some part of the world where they haven't yet thought of such things...

12

Historical Origins

I suppose this chapter should have come first; but it didn't.

The word 'catamaran' is a mis-spelled misnomer. It is derived from a Tamil word meaning literally 'lashed-logs' (i.e. a log raft, and nothing much to do with twin hulls). The term describes a small craft used, if my information is correct, for in-shore fishing in the Indian Ocean off the Coromandel Coast. Probably very wet, at that. There is a picture of one in Björn Landström's excellent book *The Ship*, showing three logs lashed tight together, the central one being the longest—more like a trimaran, really! How the name was ever given to the development of the Pacific Ocean double-canoe, I cannot discover.

The Polynesians thought up the double-canoe for off-shore voyaging, and there are many old illustrations of this sort of craft (very highly developed, too) by William Hodges who sailed with Captain Cook; by the Russian artist Louis Choris, who voyaged round the world in 1816; and away before them the Dutch explorer Tasman made some lovely sketches of double-canoes back in 1643. He shows round-bilged pairs of narrow hulls (which might or might not be trimmed to a steep 'V' under water), sporting a planked deck between them, in the middle of which is built a round-topped shelter cabin.

There seems to have been quite good bridgedeck clearance, since the hull topsides are extended somewhat in the way of the decking, so as to keep it well up off the water. One drawing by Tasman shows a *pahi*, as these voyaging canoes were sometimes called, propelled by something akin to a Lateen sail, and steered aft by two chaps with paddles and a lot of co-ordination and/or swearing as well. Woven 'claw'-sails seem to have been popular, especially when two masts of bipod construction were stepped.

It may be of interest here to note that in New Guinea there was a voyaging vessel, usually two-masted and claw-rigged, which was based not on two, but on *three* or more identical canoes, overhung and connected by decking. This was called a *lakatoi*, and is the only ancient form of long-distance sea-boat I have managed to trace which uses three separated hulls. (A similar sort of craft designed in America as an 'experimental life-saving raft', blew slowly across the Atlantic from New York in 51 days in 1867. She was called *Nonpareil*, meaning 'Match-less', and so far as I know, no one even *tried* to match her!)

Single-canoes with double-outriggers were of course commonly used for in-shore fishing from several Pacific Islands, but the passage-making travelling ships were almost invariably large versions of the *tainui* double-canoe. *Proas*, the single-outrigger canoes of which the Tongan *calie* was an especially well-developed example, were also used for long-distance sailing, again employing two hulls, though of unequal length.

I think, however, that it would be true to say that the development of the native Hawaiian double-canoe—a highly sophisticated craft with flexibly-connected hulls

215

and a single central mast, is the mother of the modern, so *wrongly* called, 'catamaran'.

Impressed by the speed and seaworthiness of the natives' twin-hulled boats sailing off Waikiki Beach back in 1937, Frenchman Eric de Bisschop built himself a 36-foot version there, named her *Kaimiloa*, and sailed her west-about and round the Cape of Storms in winter, no less, to Cannes in France.

His account, or that part of it dealing with the boat's behaviour at sea, was the inspiration which boosted the young James Wharram into action, so that he, Ruth (now Mrs Wharram) and another German girl, Jutta, became the first people ever to sail the Atlantic in both directions in a multihulled craft, and the first ever to cross the North Atlantic by catamaran. That was in their built-on-the-beach, forty-foot *Rongo*, in 1959. From *Rongo* evolved all their more recent range of designs, such as the 22-foot Hine, 34-foot Tangaroa, and so on, up to the mighty 51-foot Tehini ketch, which is very much an ocean-going sailing ship.

But I have inadvertently leapt ahead. The very first British catamaran on record is attributed appropriately (and to some maybe surprisingly) to the reign of that First British Yachtsman, H.M. King Charles II, when no less a personage than Sir William Petty was commissioned to design a double-hulled craft. This proved so successful for whatever purpose it was intended, that a second and larger version was built, which subsequently set off to cross the Atlantic by the Trade Route.

Alas, it seems that the now old catamaran bogey of 'too much weight in the hulls without the necessary strength in the connecting structure' literally proved her undoing in a Biscay storm, and she was lost. Presumably the fact was much publicised, for the idea was never repeated until Jim Wharram successfully made the same attempt in his first double boat, the alarmingly coffin-like little 23-foot *Tangaroa*. It is probably not unfair to say that his experiences in her led him to design *Rongo*, in order to sail home again. His book, *Two Girls, Two Catamarans* tells the tale.

Back to history: Over in the United States in the late 1800s, yacht designer Nathaniel Herreshoff began to toy with the twin-hulled idea. Several remarkably successful designs were constructed, and in a New York Yacht Club challenge race he sailed his best one to such effect that not a single conventional boat (however expensive) could keep anywhere near him, with the result that his 'freak' was banned from any further races.

Most of his craft were over thirty feet in length, and had elliptically shaped sections, hardly any rocker, and depended entirely on the natural grip of the long hulls to prevent leeway. Not surprisingly, for all his successes, tacking is said to have been difficult. In 1948, one of his sons, Francis L. Herreshoff, tried out some new ideas, including a very light cloth structure between the hulls (the first 'trampoline deck'), in a smaller racing cat of his own design but based on his father's boats. It went like fun but was too wet to be healthy.

For all that, we must return to Polynesia, and Hawaii in particular, for the second line of development of the cruising catamaran. Following Eric de Bisschop's 1937 *Kaimiloa*, one has to wait until shortly after the Second World War, when Woodward Brown (an ex-glider pilot) got together with Alfred Kumalai (an expert local boat-builder), and produced the forty-foot, super-light (for those days) *Manu Kai* Marconi rigged, surf-riding cata-maran. By 1955 those two had joined up with Rudy Choy, and together they turned out a second forty-footer, also built for taking trippers for thrills off the beach, and named *Waikiki Surf*. She was subsequently sailed all of 3,000 miles to America in *sixteen days*—which opened no end of ocean-racing eyes very wide indeed, and others (naturally) began to get interested. Warren Seaman then joined with Choy and Kumalai in the now famous cat-designing partnership known as CSK, whose twin-hulled ocean racers hold many a record.

In Britain, all was by no means dormant. Roland and Francis Prout were already away in the lead with their small racing cats. At the 1956 speed trials at Cowes, *Endeavour II* was timed by radar at 22 knots. Their highly successful Shearwater III Restricted Class boat (which introduced me and hundreds of others to cata-maran sailing) was later timed at 21 knots although only 16ft 6in overall.

Then came the Prouts' early cruising cats, such as *Ebb & Flo*. The Shearwater grew into a 19-foot cruising version with a lifting cabintop, and she proved so popu-lar that in months the prototype Ranger 27—to be one of the first GRP production cruising catamarans—was on their drawing board. My own *Twintail*, launched in 1965, was one of these, having sail number 34. The 45-foot Ocean Ranger, also GRP, followed then, and their Snowgoose 34 shows that the Prout Brothers' thinking is still far advanced.

By 1958 Mike Henderson's *Golden Miller*, with mast-head float and all, was saucily sailing the Solent, lifting her hulls to show her ballast keels to marine photo-graphers; but long before then, Bill O'Brien had seen what was coming, and was in there with his Jumpahead racing day-boat cat, from which hard-chine design was born the happy little 22-foot motor-sailer Shamrock. The safety aspect of cruising in this type of hard-chine cat in turn led to the 8-metre Bobcat, and his 30-foot Oceanic design became the floating home of many, and incidentally the first catamaran to sail round Cape Horn. (*Rehu Moana*, in being the first catamaran to sail round the world some five years before the Oceanic *Anneliese* made her Cape Horn trip, went in the opposite direction via the Magellan Straights.)

Many others have joined the field of cat design. In Britain, Ernie Diamond, P. M. Patterson and others produced designs for home construction, and all the while Rod Macalpine-Downie was whittling away at the racing prize-money with his uncannily quick Iroquois Mk I (*et seq.*), which was a development of *his* little racing catamaran, the *Yachting World* Cat. Tom Lack with John Winterbotham produced the Catalac as an all-out cruiser, and Pat Patterson did the same thing another way with his slightly smaller, centre-cockpit Heavenly Twins.

And so it goes on.

One thing is utterly certain. The catamaran is now a steadily growing part of the yachting scene, but for all its potential (and not infrequent) bursts of speed, I can't help feeling that, rather than as a high-performance craft, its type is going to become known better for providing the last word in efficient and really comfortable *cruising*—at least until someone dreams up an even better idea!

J. S. ANDREWS
1973

Acknowledgments

I wish to thank my Publishers, Hollis & Carter, for being understanding and very trusting. I am also grateful to the Authors and Publishers of David Lewis's *Children of Three Oceans* and Nigel Tetley's *Trimaran Solo*, from each of which I have quoted wise comments. My gratitude is also due to the authors of many books on Coastal Sailing and Ocean Voyaging from which I have learned so much —and to the writers of articles about multihulls at sea, even the unpublished ones I have had the benefit of seeing, like that by the one-time owner of *Haxted Argo II*—their information, and that derived from the pages of the AYRS reports, has been invaluable during my researches and endeavours to understand catamarans and something of their behaviour.

But above all, I sincerely want to thank Denny Desoutter, who not only checked my manuscript and cleared it of nonsenses, but who inspired it in the first place, and persuaded me to go ahead and write it.

JIM ANDREWS

Index